AF375222

For Alyssa, Theodore and Adeline.

And, of course, for Mom and Dad.

PIGEONHOLE PRODUCTIONS™

ducklings in grass

HAPPY THOUGHTS & PICTURES FOR LITTLE ONES

written & illustrated by
Gerrie Reese-Jones

bird
Look for
big and little things
in the garden.
snail

duckling

duckling

Talk with
one another.

grasshopper

butterfly
duckling

Some birds can swim
and some cannot.
That's okay.
chicks

Stay close to nature.
It's lovely.

hummingbird
dandelion seeds

There are marvels
all around.

frog
bulrushes
lily pad

Some have stronger
wings than others.

ladybug

Expect the
unexpected.

tree frog
Laugh.

Explore your
neighborhood.

dragonfly

Different creatures
can live in the same
neighborhood.
frog
worm

bee
goslings

Share your
flowers.

sunflower
daisy

Watch and listen.

Help
your
friends.
bunny

the end

LEADERSHIP SUCCESS

Expand Your Presence,
Build Trust,
and
Increase Your Influence

JEFF ROBINSON

LEADERSHIP SUCCESS

Expand Your Presence,

Build Trust,

and

Increase Your Influence

JEFF ROBINSON

To the future leaders:
May your mistakes be few,
Your successes many,
And toward the end, when you are looking back,
Your legacy be to have left things in a little
Better shape than how you found them.

TABLE OF CONTENTS

WHERE HAVE ALL THE LEADERS GONE?

I've always been known as a guy who shoots straight with people. So right here at the beginning, I'll lay out a simple truth that is so profound, we'll spend the rest of this book exploring it:

Many leaders today—even C-suite executives and others in upper management—are missing the necessary skills to be effective.

It sounds so simple, doesn't it? But when you look around at the number of ineffective organizations, frustrated employees, lost market share, and lower profits for so many companies, it shows that John Maxwell was right when he observed, "Everything rises and falls on leadership."

I'm sure we can all agree on the importance of leadership. Nothing of value happens in organizations without good leaders. Yet few people take the next step and examine what truly underpins effective leadership. Lots of people have written books on leadership, and countless talks are given on the topic. And a simple search in a standard podcast directory will show you tons of shows that focus on leadership.

The problem is that the people who need it most don't have time to read or listen to and then assimilate the vast amount of information available. Wouldn't it be great if we could just plug in and download data like they do in the Matrix movies?

Unfortunately, that's still in the realm of science fiction. As mere humans, we have to receive, analyze, and decide if information is useful, then adopt it through trial and error.

It's one thing to discover a new technique that sounds like the perfect approach as a leader. It's quite another to apply it so you can *actually lead people to accomplish a significant goal.*

Leadership coaches commonly hear questions like these:

- What skills do I need to become a more effective leader?

- What roles build more confidence as a leader?

- How can I build trust with the people I lead?

- How can I remain calm when everything is going haywire?

- How do I become a better critical thinker, and how will that affect my leadership?

Those kinds of questions are exactly why I wrote this book. I want to show you how to become a more successful, confident leader by putting my simple yet powerful framework into action. But first, let me give you a quick example of how this book can help you.

THE PATHWAY TO GREATER SUCCESS

Walter has been with his company for twenty years. Early in his career, his ambition was to become a VP or perhaps even president of the company. In the last fifteen years, he's gone from a supervisor to senior supervisor, then from manager to senior manager. Three years ago, Walter was promoted to a director role.

He is now forty-eight years old, but the VP position is still a couple of levels above him. He is beginning to lose hope that he'll ever reach that goal. Walter doesn't realize that his current skill set is the limitation that's causing his promotions to take longer than those of others who seem to have it all together.

For example, Walter doesn't have the depth and breadth of business knowledge that good leadership requires. He couldn't tell you what the accounting department does or why it's important to the overall function of the business. He doesn't see how the puzzle pieces fit together to form a cohesive picture.

Walter also struggles to stay calm under pressure. He has a reputation for losing his cool when several things come at him at once, which makes others uncomfortable. Those above him have had to soothe hurt feelings and clean up Walter's occasional messes.

He doesn't understand team dynamics or how to lead, motivate, and deploy others so they are more useful to the organization, not to mention more fulfilled and happier.

Perhaps most importantly, Walter doesn't show up with the confidence he needs to inspire other people's respect. He has no idea that other people actively avoid interacting with him and frequently talk about his poor social skills behind his back.

Walter has potential, but he needs help in several critical areas. If he were to put the material in this book into practice, he would understand:

- How to calm his mind and find his center
- How to build trust with everyone around him

- How to network with anyone in a natural and comfortable way
- How to build political capital to get promoted faster
- How to expand his understanding of the company
- How to be a lifelong learner

These skills—and more—would put Walter on a faster path to growth, satisfaction, and success. Although our example is of a nearly fifty-year-old man, the trajectory of this type of person's career isn't unique and could apply to both men and women at various stages of their careers.

WHY I WROTE THIS BOOK

Although Walter is a fictional character, his deficiencies and needs are not. Every day, millions of leaders (and aspiring leaders) in companies and organizations across the country lose out on opportunities because they are missing the crucial skills they need.

These leaders need a clear pathway to SUCCESS. The good news is that if they have the desire and ability to gain these leadership skills, they can have them!

That includes you. If the above example resonates perhaps more than you'd like to admit, you're in the right place. No matter where you are on your leadership journey, and no matter how far ahead or behind you are, you always need greater skills. We all need more SUCCESS (and as you've probably guessed, SUCCESS is not only a word, it's an acronym that I will define in these pages).

I wrote *Leadership SUCCESS* to give you a clear, compelling framework that fills a vital gap in your knowledge so you can build the skills that will elevate your life, leadership, and company.

I break down seven core competencies of leadership—for anyone who has moved up the ranks of leadership but hasn't yet developed these important skills. Maybe you have been bewildered, unclear on why you're struggling, whom to ask for help, and how to get started. As a result, you've stalled out and have failed to continue rising in responsibility and leadership.

You will get the most out of this book if you are willing and ready to improve yourself—whether it's just by reading this book or connecting with me for personal coaching (more on that later). The skills in this book are ones you can absolutely learn.

You may feel like you have already tried to move forward but something is holding you back. It isn't always easy to know what that something is.

I think of this as a closed window or sliding door. Have you seen the videos of dogs running into the glass that's just been cleaned? They think it's open, and results are painful for the dog (yet funny for everyone else). If you are open to changing yourself, the steps in this book will help you open the closed window that's been holding you back.

You don't need to move mountains to get from where you are to where you want to be. The journey to great leadership begins with small steps and new habits. That's what this book is all about—helping you discover the missing ingredient in your leadership and putting it into practice.

Before we head into Chapter One, you might be wondering, *Who is this Jeff Robinson guy, and why is he the perfect person to write this book?* Let me share a bit of my story and why I'm confident I can help you build more SUCCESS into your leadership.

HI, I'M JEFF ROBINSON!

Before I dive further into the book, it will help you to gain some personal and professional insight into who I am and what my journey has looked like.

I began to take more of an interest in leadership when I became a manager. I had a bit of a rough start because I didn't have the advantage of a good mentor. I also lacked the basic tact needed to survive in an extremely political environment. Without good guidance, I ended up learning everything the hard way.

Some of the lessons I learned were helpful, but I also picked up several poor practices that led to equally poor results. I was leading at an acceptable level, but it wasn't anywhere close to great.

Since I didn't have a good mentor, I turned to leadership books. One of my first impactful reads was Stephen R. Covey's classic, *Principle-Centered Leadership*. I realized the answers were out there—I just had to be intentional about finding them.

My passion for reading and learning about leadership came into full force as I completed my Master's of Science in Organizational Leadership from Norwich University, which fueled my fire even more.

The next step in my personal development was learning how to be a good coach, which I achieved by attaining leadership coaching certification.

For the last several years, I have grown my coaching practice alongside expanding responsibilities in my career as an organization leader.

My career journey has included a significant amount of training and consulting, both internal and external. One of the most potent lessons I've learned is that it's difficult to find people who have learned and integrated all seven core competencies of leadership. Even with all the information we have at our fingertips today, there are not enough people helping others understand how to actually be great leaders.

Having stumbled through lots of learning myself, then dedicating myself to becoming as excellent as I could be, I'm thrilled to share my knowledge with you. This book is a natural outgrowth of what I have learned and my desire to help other leaders grow and succeed.

THE ROAD AHEAD

This book is different from many other leadership books for three reasons.

First, it is grounded in the real-life principles I have not only practiced myself, but also helped other leaders to put into action.

Second, this book packs a punch quickly because I've condensed a lot of wisdom into a small number of pages. That was entirely intentional because I don't want to waste your time. In fact, I want to make great use of it. I know you're a busy leader, and I want to help you experience success sooner rather than later.

And third, it's important that you know that I'm on *your* side! As a mentor, trainer, and coach, I want you to feel safe as you apply the guidance from this book and pursue the other resources I offer. This book is the beginning link to far more than just a lecture in theory.

In Part One, we'll explore the missing ingredient of leadership: *Confidence*. I believe all your success as a leader can be boiled down to it: Either you have it or you don't.

If you lack confidence, you're stuck in what I like to call *leadership limbo*. That's why you need a coach who can help you move in the right direction and gain the confidence you need.

This leads to Part Two, where we'll dive into my SUCCESS framework. As you learn these seven elements, you'll be able to level up your leadership, understand how it can apply to your situation, and accelerate it even further.

Then in Part Three, I'll share stories of SUCCESS to help you see how this framework can work in different situations. You'll also learn how to put it into practice with a few more tips so you can become a new, more confident, bolder version of yourself as a leader.

I couldn't be more excited that you've joined me on this leadership journey. Let's begin!

THE MISSING PIECE IN LEADERSHIP

STUCK IN LEADERSHIP LIMBO

As someone who has been in manufacturing leadership for many years, I'm accustomed to dealing with equipment issues. Nothing can stop an assembly line or a production run faster than a key piece of machinery breaking down.

While you may or may not work for a manufacturing company, you've probably had the same frustrating experience with your own important piece of machinery: your car.

Have you ever been driving down the road, and all of a sudden you hear the gears *trying* to shift, but they can't? It's a terrible feeling because you realize something's wrong with the transmission.

Without a properly working transmission, you're stuck in a low gear, or perhaps no gear at all. The car can't operate as intended. You're stuck until you can get it repaired, doomed to *transportation limbo* until things are back in working order.

That's where many leaders find themselves today—stuck in *leadership limbo*. They can't move forward until they can make the proper repairs or upgrades to their skills, mindset, or connections.

THE TIDAL WAVE OF LEADERSHIP

No matter your level of leadership—whether you're brand new or you have been a leader for years—almost everyone eventually hits the closed window.

It's not hard to spot those poor results. People stop showing up to meetings. Team members leave. In nonprofit organizations, volunteers lose interest. The signs are always there, and they point to one thing: People don't feel you are leading them effectively. They may not even be able to effectively verbalize their feelings, yet the result is the same.

One of the biggest reasons why leaders stall out is the pressure. In most leadership roles, the pressure is relentless, and it feels like a tidal wave hitting you every day.

Even before you grab your first cup of coffee, fifteen or twenty different problems are waiting at your desk. Most of these arrive without warning, and if you're not prepared, it can knock you off your feet before you even get started.

I know it sounds crazy, but I've seen people walk away after just one day in a leadership role because the pressure was too much!

When you're a leader, multiple problems feel urgent in the same moment. Everyone who approaches acts like their hair is on fire, convinced the world will end if their issue isn't solved immediately. However, one of the first lessons I had to learn was simple: If everything is the hottest issue, then nothing is the hottest issue.

Thinking back through all that I've faced, I've never once had a true world-ending problem. If you don't have the right perspective, every problem or issue feels like it might be the end of the world. When you combine this with a massive lack of preparation, you are crushed under the tidal wave, and this is what keeps you stuck.

Every leader knows that the wave of problems never stops. Just like the tide, they surge in with varying intensity—sometimes crashing hard, sometimes rolling in gently—but they always keep coming.

When I was still a new leader, one of my supervisors gave me a great piece of advice. He said, "Always remember, the next crisis has already happened. It's just that nobody's told you about it yet."

I've learned that he was right. There's always another crisis waiting around the corner. The sooner you accept that reality, the less rattled you'll be.

Most people still don't know how to handle the realities of being a leader in the real world. There's an overwhelming amount of theory, and not enough practical advice.

Some companies understand the need for mentors and coaching, but their programs are often not well-designed. For example, they allow anyone to sign up as a mentor with no vetting process. Imagine being paired with a terrible leader who ends up passing along their bad habits. It happens more often than you'd think.

This is exactly why so many leaders feel lost. They are handed responsibility without training, and they are given authority without the right tools to handle it. As a result, they stay stuck.

I have seen this firsthand with my coaching clients. Over and over, I hear clients say, "Where have you been? I wish someone had explained leadership this way years ago." For many of them, all that was needed was a straightforward approach. It was the first time leadership principles had clicked in a way that made sense. This is how we develop *real leaders*, with *real skills*, who can operate in the *real world*.

LEARNING THE HARD WAY

I once worked with a young supervisor in a call center. She was in her early twenties, very capable, but nobody had ever shown her what it meant to lead. She had been promoted without training, and the only advice she'd gotten was bad.

Someone had told her, "When you take on a new group, you need to come in heavy. Be the dictator. Swing the hammer so they know you're in charge. Then you can ease up later."

She tried it, and you can probably guess how that went for her. (Hint: Not very well!)

Her people didn't respect her. They did exactly what she asked, but no more. If she gave the wrong instructions, they followed them anyway, knowing she was off base, but not caring enough to help her get it right.

Her team didn't trust her, didn't want to engage with her, and she couldn't get anything done without giving direct orders.

When this young woman came to me for coaching, she was barely surviving in her leadership. She confessed she was giving herself about another month before stepping down in her leadership role, or maybe leaving the company altogether. This was not a light decision as she'd been with her company for about five years.

We spent a great deal of time discussing the importance of respect, servant leadership, and the reality that success comes not from swinging a hammer but from building relationships. I emphasized: "Don't come in heavy. Come in friendly. In like a lamb, out like a lion. Not the other way around."

The truth is, no matter what kind of authority you think you have, you're still at the mercy of your people. Your success depends on whether or not they're willing to follow you. Good followers make good leaders. Without them, you're sunk.

As a result of my coaching, she began to change her approach. She sat down with her team and really listened. She worked on building trust instead of demanding obedience. Over time, her people started to respond differently.

She and I worked together for about a year. Roughly a year after our coaching ended, she contacted me. Not only had she survived, she'd been promoted twice. The company even asked her to start mentoring new supervisors. They believed she had the secret sauce that would help the department perform better.

Her transformation started with one simple shift: understanding that respect and trust are earned, not forced.

Once she let go of the need to prove she was in charge and started building relationships, she started to have real, meaningful success. She was no longer stuck in limbo.

LET'S MAKE IT PERSONAL

It's easy to read a case study and feel that it may not apply to your particular situation. After all, you might be in a different industry or location, with different circumstances or other factors unique to you. But the fact remains that everyone can improve their leadership skills.

To bring these principles closer to home, I've included ten questions below to help you gauge where you might be stuck in leadership limbo. As you read these questions, consider honestly whether they apply to you:

1. Do people avoid engaging with you?

2. Do you have to resort to giving orders or demanding obedience in order to get things done?

3. Do people on your team consistently make excuses for not showing up to meetings?

4. Do people under your leadership do only what is expected, but nothing more?

5. Do you view leadership as "being in charge," or do you look at it as serving and supporting?

6. Do you find yourself getting impatient when listening to your team members' problems or frustrations about their work?

7. Do you ever lose your cool or have trouble keeping your composure under pressure?

8. Do you regularly get passed over for promotions?

9. Do you sense a lack of respect from your team?

10. Do you have trouble prioritizing problems and issues?

If you answered "yes" to any of these, don't feel discouraged. We've all been there—but we're also *here* to improve our skills as leaders.

And the good news is that it's exactly why I've written this book. My goal is to get you out of leadership limbo and back on the pathway to leadership success.

CHAPTER ONE REFLECTION

Take a moment to review the ten questions in the final section of this chapter. If you could improve just one of those areas immediately, which one would it be? Why?

CHAPTER TWO

YOU NEED A CONFIDENCE COACH

Anytime you set out on a journey, you must clearly understand two things.

First, you need a firm grasp on *where you are*. Without understanding your current location, you have no idea what path to take. And second, you need someone *who has already been there*. You need a guide to show you the way.

People who climb Mount Everest don't do so alone. They have guides, called sherpas, who have climbed the mountain many times and know exactly what's required to get to the summit. The fastest and safest way to the top is by traveling with a guide.

The path to becoming an effective leader is a little like climbing Mount Everest. You have to take it step by step. There are lots of pitfalls and dangers. But most importantly, you must trust a proven guide who can assist you on your quest to reach the summit.

In Chapter One, we spent a bit of time thinking about how many leaders are stuck in "leadership limbo," that frustrating state of being where you don't seem to be making any progress. Here in Chapter Two, I want to address three misconceptions about leadership that are probably adding to your frustration.

When you zoom out and see these frustrations for what they are, it becomes obvious how much you will benefit from a guide who can show you how to build your leadership confidence.

MISCONCEPTION #1:
I DON'T HAVE NATURAL LEADERSHIP SKILLS— THEREFORE I CAN'T BE A LEADER

I see this misconception all the time. People believe that they must be outgoing, have a type A personality, possess exceptional skills, or have genius-level intelligence to be an effective leader.

Nothing could be further from the truth.

Let's go back to the analogy of climbing Mount Everest. Nobody is born with the ability to climb mountains. Instead, they must work and train to develop the variety of skills necessary for that endeavor.

Leadership works the same way. While certain people may have more natural leadership abilities, that doesn't automatically make them effective leaders. They still have to work at it. And the great news is that *anyone* can improve their leadership skills.

In fact, I've seen plenty of highly effective leaders who may not have been naturally gifted as speakers or have an outgoing personality. However, they worked hard to build their skills, worked to be highly self-aware, and in the end, they surpassed people with more natural skills.

Leadership is not a "fake it till you make it" endeavor. Faking will not get you anywhere because it lacks honesty and conceals your vulnerability. Others will respect you more when they can see that you are just as human as they are. Hard work, persistence, and understanding what skills you need will win the day, every time.

MISCONCEPTION #2
PEOPLE WILL FOLLOW ME BECAUSE OF MY TITLE

Many people believe that just because they've been given a title or position, it automatically makes them a leader. They think, *I've got the authority, so people will follow me.*

The reality is that the title doesn't guarantee much of anything except that you'll be invited to meetings. Leadership has very little to do with a job description. It has everything to do with how you actually show up and whether you've built the skills to lead.

John Maxwell famously said, "The loyalty of followers comes as a reward for the leader who earns it." You must show people you care about them and want them to be successful. The building blocks of your success as a leader are the successes of your team.

Leadership is about relationships. To build better relationships, you need to break it down into skills you can practice and improve. It helps tremendously to have a coach who can say, "Here's what you're struggling with, and here are a few steps to work on." With the right guidance, you can pick up those skills quickly.

Without those skills, you end up on what I call the twenty-five-year plan—slowly figuring things out through trial and error, sometimes right at the end of your career when it's too late to fully benefit.

As a coach, my goal is to shorten your learning curve. I'm here to help you find the most direct path from where you are now to the summit of your leadership potential.

MISCONCEPTION #3
I MUST DO EVERYTHING MYSELF

A final misconception is the idea that leaders must carry the whole burden alone. They confuse accountability with responsibility. Just because you're the leader doesn't mean you have to do everything yourself.

Leadership is about the team. It's about building your inner circle, leaning on the people around you, and figuring out how to move forward together.

If you try to show up as the one with all the answers, it usually backfires. People don't actually respect you more when you act like you know it all. They respect you when you're willing to say, "I'm not sure," or "I don't know—can you help me?"

That kind of humility opens doors that pride keeps shut.

Most people don't want to admit they need help. They're afraid it will make them look weak or unqualified. But in my experience, very few people will resist you if you come to them honestly and say, "I need help." No matter how tough they act, or even if you've had conflict in the past, most people will lower their defenses when you ask for assistance in a genuine way.

That simple phrase—"I need help"—is one of the most underrated strategies for building trust and connection. It creates respect and strengthens relationships far more than pretending you can carry everything on your own.

Here's something else to consider: If you look at the lives of highly successful people, there's a common thread. They have the humility to ask for help. Even when they're starting out with no credibility, with no right to be asking for a favor, they go ahead and do it anyway.

And a surprising number of times, they got what they wanted—simply because they asked.

WHY DO LEADERS STRUGGLE WITH CONFIDENCE?

I could add a lot more to the list of leadership misconceptions, but the three I've identified in this chapter are a great starting point. I'm sure you can add your own items to the list.

All of this begs the question, "Why do leaders struggle so much to build confidence and be successful?" I believe a big part of it is plain old frustration. Leaders realize they're not getting the results they want, but they don't know why, or what to do next. They know something needs to change, but they don't have the answers and they don't always know whom to ask. Or maybe they're not willing to ask.

We all struggle to make progress in areas that are important to us because we don't know what we don't know. We don't have a map to help us get there ... and we may not know who has the map.

That's exactly what brought you to this book. You came here looking for answers to your leadership problem. You want more success as a leader. You're looking for someone who's already walked the path and can point out the dangers, shortcuts, and signposts.

As I mentioned earlier, my goal here is to be that kind of resource for you. Most folks don't take time to read leadership books, attend conferences, listen to podcasts, and consume other resources. But I do.

At the end of the day, your very best resource is to team up with another live human being who understands your situation and can help you find your specific, personalized path. We'll talk more about what that process looks like later in the book, especially as we dive into my SUCCESS framework in Part Two.

For now, I'll conclude this chapter with a quick tip that can help you start getting leadership results immediately. You'll see a few of these tips sprinkled throughout the book. This tip is one of my favorites!

JEFF'S LEADERSHIP TIP #1:
STRESS IS A CHOICE

Most of the time, a lack of confidence doesn't come from not knowing the answer. It comes from not knowing how to approach the problem in front of you. Maybe it sounds a bit discouraging, but we almost never have the answer the first time something shows up. That's okay.

What matters is stepping back and recognizing the situation for what it is: a problem. Then we begin working through a solution. The basics of problem-solving are always the same. You take what information you have, break down the problem, and figure out a solution.

In science, that's called forming a hypothesis. In business, a simple version is the "plan–do–check–act" cycle that was popularized by W. Edward Demings in the 1950s. You make a plan, you do it, you check and study your results, and then you act on what you've learned.

It's not about perfection; it's about steady progress.

When you frame problems that way, they stop feeling overwhelming. Stress comes when you let the situation confuse you or make you feel trapped. But in day-to-day leadership, you always have the choice to *not be stressed.*

Before you object to what I'm saying, I realize that some people are more prone to anxiety than others. Telling them "Don't be stressed" can actually make them more stressed! Sometimes it takes time, coaching, and practice to reframe things.

But here's the reality of leadership: People don't come to you just for answers. They come to see how calm you are. If you're calm, they'll follow. If you lose your composure, so will they.

You face the same problem regardless of whether you are calm or stressed out. If you choose stress, you have to solve the problem with half of your available brain power, because the stress is using up the rest. You get to make the choice between stress and calm.

Giving in to stress and failing to remain calm is only one of the potential pitfalls of the leadership journey. It's why confidence, and becoming more successful as a whole, is so vital.

Before we move on to Part Two, where we'll explore my SUCCESS framework, we'll take a quick look at the hidden costs of staying where you are as a leader. It's important to realize just what it's costing if you choose *not* to grow. That's the topic of Chapter Three.

CHAPTER TWO REFLECTION

In this chapter, we explored three misconceptions about leadership:

1. I don't have natural leadership skills—therefore I can't be a leader.

2. People will follow me because of my title.

3. I must do everything myself.

Which of these misconceptions do you wrestle with the most in your leadership? (Be honest.) And how do you imagine a leadership coach could help you make incredible progress in this area?

THE HIDDEN COST OF STAYING WHERE YOU ARE

Everything has a price.

This shouldn't come as a surprise. Anytime you want something in life, there is an associated cost.

If you go to the grocery store, you have to pay. If you want a new car, you have to pay. If you want an education, you have to pay. If you want to see a doctor or take a prescription, you have to pay.

Everything in life *costs something*. You may not always pay in dollars, but rest assured, you will pay.

That's true of leadership as well. If you want to move forward with your goals or get a promotion, it will cost you time, effort, discipline, and attention. But make no mistake, it also costs you something to *stay where you are.*

That's right—everything has a price, including doing nothing. That's why, in this chapter, I want to spell out several ways you will pay if you continue your present course of action and do nothing to improve your leadership.

It's natural to want to stay comfortable, but it doesn't mean that's where you need to stay. Our natural tendency as humans is to avoid pain and suffering. That's why so many people don't exercise, read books, or improve their career prospects.

But if you stay where you are in leadership, that costs something, too. You'll eventually pay a hefty price if you ignore your opportunities to grow. I put all these in the category of "hidden" costs because many people don't realize how much their lack of growth is costing them. I'll frame these as questions. Then at the end of the chapter, I'll challenge you with some thoughts on the opportunity cost of leadership and give you another success tip.

ARE YOU LETTING DOWN YOUR FOLLOWERS?

The greatest hidden cost of staying where you are as a leader shows up in your followers. I know that sounds counterintuitive, because our human tendency is to think of ourselves first.

But if you're not growing, improving, and learning, *the people you lead are the ones who pay the price.*

I believe your primary responsibility as a leader is not the numbers, the production schedule, or the quotas. Those things matter, of course, but they're not the main thing.

Your main job is to take care of your people. They're the ones who will get the results, recruit others, and bring the numbers up. Without strong, healthy followers, nothing else works and nothing else really matters.

That's why this hidden cost is so dangerous. When you fail to develop yourself, your team doesn't receive the leadership they need. They miss goals. They get discouraged. They start to feel like they're not supported. They will eventually leave if they have the opportunity. And even worse, the best workers leave first!

I'm always careful about using the word *fail* because the word feels ugly to most folks. People seldom fail outright. They may fall short, miss targets, or get unfavorable results. But they learn from those experiences—or at least they should. And when learning happens, the experience is no longer a total failure.

As one of my clients noted, "If no one lost a limb, we didn't fail."

If you stay stuck, you create an environment where your followers stay stuck, too. And the worst part is, most of the time they won't tell you straight out. They'll just disengage quietly. They'll stop showing up with their full efforts. Sooner or later, they'll walk away.

That's the most important cost of not growing as a leader. Not dollars, not hours, but good people slipping through your fingers because they never received the leadership they needed from you.

ARE YOU COMPROMISING YOUR PERSONAL GROWTH?

Another hidden cost of staying where you are is the impact on your own personal growth. If you're not learning and improving, you're going to stunt your own development.

In fact, you might even start to convince yourself that you're not cut out for leadership at all.

This is where the cycle begins. You feel like you're failing, you don't know how to break out of it, and before long, you've built your own psychological prison. You keep running into the same problems, getting the same poor results, and beating yourself up for not being able to change things.

That sense of frustration doesn't just go away—it builds over time. And it's absolutely maddening.

On a career level, the cost is just as high. If you're in a leadership role and you stop growing, your career stalls out. You hit the closed window and can't get it open. Other people around you start getting promoted, while you stay in place. It doesn't take very long before your organization begins to label you as the guy or gal who is a good worker but who has no potential for further growth.

Once the higher-ups start seeing you as someone who's reached their ceiling, changing their minds is hard. You get pigeonholed and are no longer seen as someone with potential. And in many cases, you can stay stuck in that place for years.

That's why personal growth isn't optional. If you want to move forward in leadership—and in life—you have to keep learning. Otherwise, it costs your future.

It's not just the opportunities you lose. It's also the chance to become the kind of leader you were meant to be.

ARE YOU STUCK IN YOUR CAREER?

Another hidden cost of staying where you are shows up in your career. Let's say you've been promoted to supervisor, first-level manager, or even mid-level management. You're doing okay and the work is getting done. Your team shows up, hits the targets, and the operation keeps moving. On paper, everything looks fine.

But here's the problem: It's never exceptional. You never have those standout moments that set you and your team apart.

Without those moments, the people above you eventually start to see you as someone who has plateaued.

They are probably thinking, *We're getting what we need from this person, but they're not strong enough to move higher.* That perception can lock you in place and prevent you from moving up the ladder.

Another way this shows up is when folks come into coaching saying, "They won't promote me." What that usually means is that the people seeking coaching have hit a plateau and don't understand why.

They are usually blaming upper management, their colleagues, or other circumstances rather than seeing that they are holding themselves back.

Sometimes the problem is that people don't realize what good leadership actually looks like. They've been modeling themselves after bad leaders, and they don't even know it.

I've talked to people halfway through their careers who finally encountered a truly good leader for the first time. Their reaction is usually the same: "I had no idea how bad I was until now." When they finally see the difference, it's like a lightbulb goes on.

Now that I've helped you think about three ways that staying where you are might be costing you, let's zoom out a bit as I share a few thoughts on the different prices every leader must choose for themselves.

COUNTING THE OPPORTUNITY COSTS OF LEADERSHIP

For the most part, climbing the leadership ladder requires a focus on your career, which means you will struggle to have the same level of focus on other things, including family. I rarely hear this talked about in leadership circles. Whether you are focused on your family or a career, there is absolutely a cost.

Those who chose this career have paid deeply. They won't be at every ball game. They will miss opportunities to coach their kids' teams. They might be on the road during a graduation or birthday. They provide more financially, but often at the expense of being fully present at home.

That's why I tell new leaders to decide up front which path you're taking. But remember, you can always adjust. You're not stuck with your first choice, but you should be conscious of the trade-offs. Everything has a price.

It all depends on what you want out of life. Having worked with both—people who choose a family focus and those who are career focused—I respect whatever choice someone wants to make (in essence, whatever price they choose to pay), but I want them (and you) to make that choice intentionally.

Far too many people don't know what they want out of life. So they go through their days, years, or even decades without stopping to consider what they truly desire or what price it will require. I don't want that to happen to you.

Before I conclude this chapter, let's take a quick break for another leadership tip you can put into practice right away.

JEFF'S LEADERSHIP TIP #2:
THE POWER OF SELF-AWARENESS

I'll get straight to the point. If you feel like you're stuck, you probably are. And it's probably not others who are holding you back—it's you.

So how do you move forward? With the power of self-awareness.

Self-awareness is one of the most powerful tools you can develop as a leader. It means stepping back, being honest with yourself, and looking at your behavior through the lens of other people. For example, consider how the situation looks to your leader (first lens), your peers (second lens), your team (third lens), and your inner circle or coach (fourth lens).

How do they see you? What habits or attitudes might be keeping you from moving forward?

A lack of self-awareness shows up in different ways. For some people, it's overconfidence. This usually shows up as arrogance, egotism, or entitlement—acting like you've already arrived when you haven't. For others, it's the opposite. They don't have much confidence and don't have a clue why things aren't working.

Both extremes are equally damaging, and both come from the same root problem: not knowing yourself well enough.

If you don't know how you're showing up, you can't make changes. You'll either keep pushing people away with arrogance or you'll continue to sell yourself short because you don't realize your own blind spots.

That's why building self-awareness isn't optional—it's essential. Becoming more self-aware is what lets you see the barriers (aka limiting beliefs) you've put in your own path, and then take responsibility for removing them.

The more aware you are, the better chance you have of breaking free from being stuck and moving forward as the kind of leader others actually want to follow.

That leads us directly into Part Two, where I'll share the solution you've been looking for on your journey to become a leader who is a true SUCCESS!

CHAPTER THREE REFLECTION

As you consider various ways that staying where you are might be costing you, look back over your career. Have you paid any of these prices in the past? Which ones are you paying right now, and what is it costing you in terms of career growth and opportunities?

PART TWO

THE SOLUTION YOU'VE BEEN SEARCHING FOR

A FRAMEWORK TO LEVEL UP YOUR LEADERSHIP

In Part One, we explored what's missing in your leadership. Since you're still reading this book, you probably relate to being in leadership limbo. That's why you need a coach—a guide who can help you navigate the turbulent waters of leading other people.

The compass we'll use is my seven-part SUCCESS framework. Each of the seven letters stands for a vital category you must develop as a leader. In this chapter, I'll provide a brief overview of each component and explain why it is crucial to your leadership.

However, first, let me share a bit about where this system originated and what makes it unique.

WHAT MAKES THIS FRAMEWORK UNIQUE?

Many leaders are trained on processes—how to improve a system, how to streamline steps, how to fix bottlenecks—but they aren't being trained how to lead the people who have to carry out those processes.

If you don't have people who can lead the team members doing the work, everything falls apart. You can be taught the best process in the world, but if you don't know how to lead people through the changes, you'll fail. Leadership bridges the gap between good ideas and real results.

> LEADERSHIP BRIDGES THE GAP BETWEEN GOOD IDEAS AND REAL RESULTS.

That realization is what eventually shaped my approach to leadership and led me to develop the SUCCESS framework. It is based on the questions my clients have asked most often. I developed it by working through each subject with the people who were hitting the closed window.

For example, one of the first closed windows I had to personally navigate was realizing how important rapport and self-awareness are. If you can't build trust with your team, or you're blind to how you're treating them, you're going to get poor results.

That's exactly what happened to me. It really hit home the first time I took a personality profile. The gentleman who reviewed it told me, "Jeff, you'll always get the job done, but you don't care how many bodies you stack up along the way. If you don't fix that, nobody will ever trust you."

I was stunned by this comment, and it stuck with me. I went through several levels of learning to understand that leadership isn't about treating people like parts of a machine. They're not a herd of cattle, and they're not nameless resources. They're real people. This is just one of the lessons that led to a framework that will accelerate your path.

That is what makes the SUCCESS framework so effective and work so well. It's not just leadership theory. It is a system created from years of experience and practical application that can help anyone adapt to their personality quirks, blind spots, and the areas where growth is needed. And yes, it can help anyone, including *you*.

To put it simply, this is a leadership framework developed for you to use successfully—and it has been demonstrated across hundreds of coaching hours.

Now, let's take a closer look at each of the seven components of the framework.

S – STEADFAST CHARACTER

Steadfast character is all about *building reliability*.

Why? Because the foundation of great leadership is character that doesn't waver when the pressure comes. Being steadfast doesn't mean you never feel doubt, but it does mean you've built the inner strength to handle whatever comes your way.

One of the keys to being steadfast is choosing which *inner voice* you listen to. We all have an inner critic that whispers negativity and feeds fear. But we also have an inner advocate—the voice that supports us, pushes us, and reminds us we are capable.

Your inner advocate doesn't sugarcoat things; it helps you adjust when you drift off course. It's committed to your well-being, persistent in helping you succeed, and compassionate enough to listen to your doubts without letting them take over.

As a leader, you have to learn to hear your advocate. When you reflect on something, listen for the voice of someone (your spouse, a friend, a child) who always supports you and focus on that instead of the doubt.

Another element of becoming steadfast is having perspective of what is truly at stake in any given situation. Remember, you don't carry the fate of the world on your shoulders. Don't let every situation whip you up into panic. Take one thing at a time and keep decisions in their proper scale.

Take time to establish a *reset point*—a mental space that brings calm and clarity. The Dhammapada says, "Within you there is a stillness and sanctuary to which you can retreat at any time and be yourself."

Here is how to find your reset point:

Think of something you do where the focus is so complete that everything else melts away—whether it's jogging, baking, mowing the lawn, reading, floating in the pool, or anything that just lets you completely relax.

- Close your eyes and take yourself there now.

- Describe where you are.

- What can you hear?

- What can you see?

- What can you smell?

- What are you feeling?

- As soon as you feel completely at peace, take a mental photograph.

You can retreat to this picture anytime you need to, even if it's only for a few seconds.

I also encourage you to practice self-gratitude as part of your quest to become more steadfast. I like to use an exercise called "Three Pats on the Back."

- Schedule fifteen minutes toward the end of each day.

- Think about your day and identify three good things you did. They don't have to be earth-shattering. Maybe you encouraged someone, solved a small problem, or kept your cool in a tough moment.

- Write them down.

- Take a minute to reflect on them and give yourself some gratitude for them.

Over time, this habit of patting yourself on the back rewires your perspective. Instead of focusing on the negatives, you start to see yourself as capable, steady, and strong. These are the exact qualities your team needs in a leader.

U – UNRELENTING TRUST

Unrelenting trust is all about *strengthening relationships.*

Trust is the foundation of all leadership. Nothing of real value can happen without it. You can have the best ideas, the sharpest strategies, and the loftiest goals, but if the people around you don't trust you or you don't trust them, progress will always stall out.

You don't want to strive for just *trust*, however; you want to build *unrelenting* trust. This means developing a deep, steadfast belief in your team such that when things seem difficult and messed up, you truly know they are doing their best without ill intentions. And if you show them authenticity, they will return the same level of trust.

Why? Because when trust is present, you can build momentum quickly and maintain it. People lean in and work harder because they believe in you.

Steven M. R. Covey famously said trust is built on two things: character and competence. Character means walking your talk—doing what you say you'll do and living by the values you claim to hold. Competence means being capable in your role and willing to admit when you don't have the answer.

Sometimes leaders break trust with their followers—not because they lack skills, but because they pretend to know what they don't. Your team will respect your honesty far more than a false front.

If trust has been strained, you can't ignore it—you must face it head-on. Be vulnerable enough to admit there's a problem. Ask for feedback. Then listen without reacting defensively. That's the moment when healing begins.

You may need to swallow your pride, apologize, or "fall on your sword" to make things right. Over time, the feedback will let you know trust is being rebuilt. As Jack Welch once said, "You'll know it when you feel it."

It's also vital that you do your best to be transparent. When you're not sure about something, tell people, "I don't have the answer yet, but I'm confident we can figure it out together. Once we have a plan, I'll make sure we have the resources to carry it through."

That kind of honesty is very reassuring to your team. They don't expect perfection. What they need is a leader they can count on—someone who builds trust by being open and consistent in their words and actions.

C – C.A.L.M.

Calm is all about *bringing stability.*

One of the first lessons I had to learn in management was how to stay calm when everything around me was falling apart. I'll never forget one Monday morning early in my career. I had barely set my bag down when an employee told me her daycare had called. Her child was sick, and she needed to leave.

Moments later, the production control manager rushed in, rattling off a list of part numbers—critical items we needed to track down immediately to keep the production line moving. Then the facilities manager called about a machine that had suddenly gone down and needed urgent attention. And before I could even open my inbox, my boss had already requested new slides for a 1:00 p.m. meeting. Welcome to being a leader! Sometimes the only constant element in leadership is the presence of chaos. In moments like this, your ability to stay calm makes the difference between survival and burnout.

Dawn Steel wrote an autobiography titled *They Can Kill You but They Can't Eat You.* Her figurative point is since you can't be eaten, there is no point in killing you. I have used this phrase for years to remind myself to keep things in perspective. And that perspective is: *Nothing is so important that you need to lose your mind over it.* **No matter what it is, take a breath, square up your shoulders, and take care of it.**

> NOTHING IS SO IMPORTANT THAT YOU NEED TO LOSE YOUR MIND OVER IT.

Every time that I'm faced with a bunch of problems at once, I ask myself, *Does this problem mean the world is about to end?* If not, then I can take a breath and find my center. (Hint: The world has never ended because of a problem I've faced.)

When you let your emotions hijack your thinking, you end up thrashing around instead of leading with confidence.

I picture my mind as a pool of water. If the surface is choppy, I don't wade in until it's still. Once I feel calm, I can apply a simple four-step process using the letters of C.A.L.M.:

- **C**enter in on one problem. Stop trying to solve everything at once, and pick the first priority.

- **A**ssess the information you already have. It may not be complete, but it's a starting point.

- **L**ook at your options and weigh the risks of each one.

- **M**ove forward with the best choice you can make right now.

It sounds simple, but it works. Staying calm doesn't eliminate chaos, but it does give you clarity. And that is exactly what your team needs most in the middle of a crisis.

C – COLLABORATION AND DELEGATION

Collaboration and delegation are all about *empowering teams.*

One of the biggest turning points for any leader is learning to let go. Often, it feels easier to just do the work yourself. You know exactly how you want things done, and explaining it to someone else takes time you think you don't have.

But leadership isn't about holding on to every task. When you collaborate with others and practice good delegation, you multiply your influence and empower your team.

Effective delegation is a combination of strength and risk assessment. It begins with understanding your team members. What are their strengths? What's already on their plate? Is the task something they can do easily, or will it stretch them in a healthy way?

Then you must assess the risk of a poor outcome. If they miss the mark, how many people would be affected? How much money could it cost? How much of your time would be needed to clean it up?

Delegation isn't all-or-nothing—it happens at different levels. At the lowest level, you might say, "Do this exactly as I show you and report back." At the next level, you could assign several tasks and ask just for routine updates. And at the highest level, you might hand off a project entirely and ask only for the outcome. The key is to set clear expectations, agree on a timeline, and be available for questions without hovering.

When you delegate well, you're not just lightening your load. You are creating teachable moments. Every task you pass on is a chance for someone else to learn, grow, and gain confidence. That is collaboration at its best: You give direction and protection, and your team gets to learn new skills and feel more ownership.

After all, you are only credible as a leader insofar as your people are successful. When they win, you win. You don't have to carry everything yourself. Trust your team, delegate wisely, and watch them rise to the occasion.

> *TRUST YOUR TEAM, DELEGATE WISELY, AND WATCH THEM RISE TO THE OCCASION.*

E – EXECUTIVE PRESENCE

Executive presence is all about *commanding respect.*

It's not just about trying to look confident and "in charge" at a meeting, or giving a polished presentation. Presence is a blend of credibility, calm, and authenticity that helps people see they can trust you as a leader. When you walk into a room, people can immediately sense whether you command respect or you're trying to fake it.

One of the strongest ways to build executive presence is through active listening. Many people believe they need to prove their intelligence by talking excessively. The opposite is actually true. Credibility comes from listening carefully, understanding the context, and speaking only when you have something valuable to say.

Another element of executive presence is emotional intelligence. Many books have been written about this topic. It means being aware of your thoughts and emotions, then regulating them instead of letting them spill out. It's about reading others well enough to meet them where they are. Emotions are tools, so use them wisely.

Appearance and etiquette are important. People notice how you dress, groom, and carry yourself. You don't need to be flashy—in fact, blending in appropriately works best. But you do need to look like someone who takes the role seriously.

When you combine listening, emotional intelligence, and a professional image, you project the confidence and steadiness that your people need.

I'll also add that strategic networking is vital to good leadership. In many ways, success is based on the relationships you build. Teach yourself to see everyone as an opportunity to expand your knowledge and influence. To break the ice with a new person, approach them with sincere curiosity about who they are, what they do, and the things they like. They will remember that you were interested in them.

Political capital is the goodwill you build with influential people. As a leader, you rely on others to achieve your goals and sometimes, you ask them to do something simply because it is you who is asking. This works only if they trust you and you've taken time to build a strong relationship.

Realize that political capital goes both ways. As you build a strong presence, you will be approached by others. Loan your influence to them carefully. If someone deserves help, give it. But remember, what they do will reflect on you, so make sure it gives a good reflection.

If you take the time to use all of the elements of executive presence together, you will become the person who gets things done with integrity. The respect this brings is a cornerstone of successful leadership.

S – SAVVY BUSINESS ACUMEN

Savvy business acumen is all about *making smart decisions.*

Strong leaders do more than manage people. They understand the big picture of the business itself. When you know how your work connects to other functions, you make smarter decisions, avoid costly mistakes, and gain the respect of your peers and the people above you.

Building this kind of awareness requires both a breadth and depth of business knowledge. Breadth means understanding how the various departments within the company work together, including operations, sales, finance, HR, and more. Depth means having a clear understanding of your own area and how it drives results for the entire company. You need both elements.

I encourage you to read annual reports, financial statements, and industry news to stay informed. Pay attention to business media. Volunteer for cross-functional teams, where you'll see firsthand how decisions affect different parts of the organization.

Also, don't underestimate casual learning such as lunch discussions, coffee chats, or even a quick question after a meeting. These can all expand your understanding in meaningful ways.

Just like its importance in executive presence, networking is a critical piece of becoming savvier. Great leaders know it's all about who you know. But I'm not talking about using people to get what you want. Instead, truly great networking is all about curiosity and connection.

Ask thoughtful questions, make conversations about the other person, and care enough to remember what they tell you. Be ready to explain who you are and what you do. Be mindful of adjusting your approach to fit your audience instead of sounding too rehearsed.

If you want to build your business acumen, it will take time but it's absolutely worth it.

S – SELF-DEVELOPMENT

Self-development is all about *fueling continuous growth.*

Great leaders never stop learning. Self-development is not an optional add-on to your career. It's a huge part of the job. If you want to grow, you must be intentional about building knowledge, skills, and perspective.

The key is to find a method that works for you. Some people thrive on reading books, magazines, or articles. Others prefer listening—podcasts, audiobooks, TED Talks, or similar material during a commute. And some people would rather watch YouTube videos or read blogs.

The medium doesn't matter as much as the consistency. Choose the format that fits your lifestyle so you'll actually stick with it.

The most important thing in self-development is to schedule time for it, just like you would do with any other important responsibility. Block out time for it each day or week. Maybe it's fifteen or twenty minutes a day or two hours per week. Treat it like it's non-negotiable, because it is—if you want to keep growing as a leader.

One of the best ways to truly learn material you're absorbing is to teach it to other people. When you share insights with your team, lead a book club, or present what you've discovered at a meeting, it forces you to process the material on a deeper level.

Over time, people begin to see you as a subject-matter expert, which builds both your confidence and your credibility. It's honestly one of the reasons I love being a coach. Not only do I get to help many others, but I also become better myself because I'm teaching what I'm learning.

Self-development is fuel for continuous growth. The more you learn, the more prepared you'll be to guide others. Leaders who stop learning eventually stop leading.

> *LEADERS WHO STOP LEARNING EVENTUALLY STOP LEADING.*

The seven steps of the SUCCESS model are not all-inclusive of every challenge a leader faces. They address the most common challenges that people have asked me for help with. And focusing on these seven aspects will help any leader be much more effective, which leads to a more enjoyable and satisfying workplace.

In the next chapter, I'll help you take what you've learned so far and apply it directly to your leadership situation. After all, everyone's leadership context is different. You can start applying these principles right now, right where you are. I'll show you how in Chapter Five.

CHAPTER FOUR REFLECTION

In previous reflections, I have asked you to consider how the material applies to your own leadership. This time, think about the best leader you've ever worked for. How did he or she display each of these seven qualities? How did their effective leadership help you to do your job better and reach your potential?

YES, SUCCESS CAN WORK FOR YOU

Now that you have a handle on the SUCCESS framework and what it's all about, let's take it a step further. You're probably wondering what it looks like in action and whether it can actually apply to your situation.

In this chapter, I'll share a quick story about a leader who used this system to experience an incredible breakthrough. Then we'll explore a secret to getting results, one you rarely hear mentioned in leadership circles. And finally, we'll wrap up the chapter with another practical leadership tip.

OPENING THE WINDOW

One of my favorite clients was a man who had spent decades in engineering leadership. By the time he came to me, he was well into the latter part of his career. He kept hitting what felt like the same closed window over and over again. After years of frustration, he'd almost given up on ever achieving success.

During one of our early conversations, he admitted that people often described him as intimidating. He blurted out, "They say I'm gruff, but I don't really understand what that means. I'm just giving them the facts. I tell it like it is and expect people to move forward with the information."

From his perspective, he was just doing his job. But to the people around him, his approach came across as overly harsh and insensitive.

The word that kept coming up in feedback from others was *rigid*. Everyone seemed to use it, but he didn't know what to do with it. One day he got frustrated and asked, "What does that even mean? Everybody calls me rigid, but I don't get it."

That moment opened the door for some powerful coaching. We worked together to unpack what other people were telling him when they used that word. I explained that being rigid meant that he didn't bend—he was so entrenched in his way of doing things that he made other people feel dismissed or shut down.

It wasn't about his technical competence. It was about how people experienced him.

It was a real turning point in his journey. For the first time in his career, he started to see himself through the eyes of others. As we worked through the SUCCESS framework, he became more self-aware and started to recognize the moments when his harsh tone was shutting down good communication.

Over time, this leader learned how to listen differently. He also built skills in acknowledging other people's perspectives and adjusting his approach when needed. Even better, he started to lean into feedback and became more approachable.

By opening the window, he had discovered new tools and skills for connecting with people and having real influence—all because someone had helped him translate feedback into real action that had a huge impact on his leadership.

A LITTLE-KNOWN SECRET TO GETTING RESULTS

Here's one of the biggest ironies of leadership: Most of the breakthroughs you're searching for aren't *out there somewhere waiting for you—they're already inside you.* The challenge is learning how to discover them.

This is where coaching comes in. Coaching is about challenging assumptions, especially the ones we don't realize we're making.

For example, if I tell you, "You're rigid, and I don't like working with you," I'm assuming you know exactly what I mean. But maybe you don't. You might hear "rigid" and think I mean that you are too hard on people, when I actually mean you're inflexible. We could walk away with two completely different understandings of the same word.

The SUCCESS framework helps you unpack these assumptions. It creates space to ask questions like:

- What does this feedback actually mean?

- How do the people around me actually see me?

- Where is the gap between my intention as a leader and the experience of my followers?

Once you start asking those questions, you realize something powerful: Almost every leadership challenge begins with *you*.

That might feel pretty discouraging at first. Nobody likes to think they're the problem. But here's the surprising twist: If the problem really is about you, that means you have the power to do something about it. In other words, it's the best answer you can hope for!

You're not at the mercy of the world, your team, or your circumstances. You're in the driver's seat. It doesn't mean other people don't contribute to the problem. Of course they do. But you are never completely powerless. The moment you take ownership and identify what you can do to improve the situation, you start to shift the outcome.

DO YOU WANT TO ACCELERATE YOUR SUCCESS?

Whenever I tell stories about people I have helped, a common response is, "Well, that worked for them, but my situation is different." We all believe our challenges are unique. After all, you are the one living them every day, with all the details and emotions attached.

Your situation might be unique, but your problems are not. Every leader I've worked with has wrestled with the same kinds of issues.

Are you struggling with a difficult employee who doesn't play well with others? You're not alone. Are you feeling blocked in your own head, wondering why you aren't being promoted? That's pretty common. Are you fighting against the nagging belief that you don't have enough experience yet? I've heard that one many times.

The challenges repeat themselves, even though the specifics might be different according to the industry or company.

The part that is unique, however, *is your pathway forward.* The road you take to move past those problems is yours, and nobody else's. No two leadership journeys look the same, which is why it's so important to have a coach who can help you navigate the terrain.

Sure, you could figure things out on your own. Most people eventually do. But here's the catch—it could take you ten or twenty years. By the time you finally piece it together, you may be at the end of your career, looking back and wishing you'd had a breakthrough much earlier.

Working with a guide shortens the path. You don't waste decades circling around the same obstacles over and over. Instead, you learn to see them for what they are, then deal with them and move forward.

That is the power of the SUCCESS framework. It doesn't magically erase your challenges, but it gives you a structure to face them directly, with support and clarity, so you can make progress right now instead of years down the road.

If you are feeling skeptical, it's okay. But don't let that skepticism keep you stuck. Your problems are not new, and they're not insurmountable.

The only real question is this: Will you keep trying to figure it out the hard way, or will you choose to walk a faster, more intentional path forward.

Before I wrap up this chapter, I'd love to share another leadership tip you can start using today.

JEFF'S LEADERSHIP TIP #3:
TAKE SMALL STEPS

Let me expand on a principle I mentioned earlier in this chapter. One of the biggest mistakes I see leaders make is assuming that other people are always responsible for their problems.

The moment you say, "It's out of my hands," you've given away your power. You've surrendered your ability to make positive changes. But in reality, the situation is never completely outside your control.

There is *always* some part of the problem you can influence.

It doesn't take a massive shift to create meaningful change. Lots of leaders get stuck because they think they have to move mountains to accomplish something worthwhile. It feels impossible, so they don't even try.

As Malcom Gladwell points out in his book *The Tipping Point*, progress builds up slowly, from small adjustments, until one tiny shift pushes everything forward.

You don't have to change the whole world. You just need to take the first step. Take networking, for example. Many people avoid it because they don't feel confident striking up conversations. They imagine they need to suddenly become a huge extrovert who can effortlessly talk to anyone.

That feels completely overwhelming to most people, so they quit before they start. It's not necessary for you to become a world-class networker overnight. Instead, set a small goal like this: Over the next month, introduce yourself to three people you don't know and ask them a question.

The question doesn't have to be profound. It can be as simple as, "How long have you been with this company?" or "What do you like most about your role?" What matters most is that you prove to yourself you can initiate the conversation. Each small success builds confidence. Pretty soon, you realize the world is opening up in ways you never expected.

Don't wait for a big, dramatic moment to improve your leadership. Protect your power by taking ownership of the small steps right in front of you. In the next chapter, we'll explore what it means to take even greater ownership by accelerating your leadership success.

CHAPER FIVE REFLECTION

In this chapter, I've challenged you to consider how the SUCCESS framework could help you, no matter your circumstances. I shared the story of a leader who applied it and experienced a remarkable breakthrough. Consider what your situation could be like one year from now if you had a similar breakthrough. What would it feel like to move past the obstacles that have held you back? Be specific.

THE BEST WAY TO ACCELERATE YOUR SUCCESS

You've heard the phrase, "Don't judge a book by its cover." But just like most people, you probably judged this book by its cover.

When you saw the design, I hope you had a very positive reaction! The graphic designer who created the cover and the interior layout worked hard and did a fantastic job, wouldn't you agree?

There is another aspect to this book you might have judged, though. Whether you picked up a print copy of *Leadership SUCCESS* or are reading it in a digital format, you probably noticed that it's a short book. You might have thought, "Surely this book can't be all that valuable because it's so short!"

As they say, good things come in small packages. That's certainly my hope and intention for this book. But let me explain a bit further.

You see, I didn't set out to give you all the answers or solve every possible problem related to leadership in this book. It's easy to pick up a big book and assume that if you just read it, your problems will magically solve themselves.

I had a different goal with *Leadership SUCCESS*. I wanted to give you enough practical value that you could put it into practice immediately and begin seeing results right away. But even more importantly, my goal was to give you the most powerful solution possible—the solution that, if you implement it, will skyrocket your results faster than simply reading a book could ever do.

Let's explore a bit more.

YOU NEED A *WHO*, NOT A *HOW*

When leaders feel stuck, their first instinct is often to seek more information. I understand this because I love to read. Every year, I read dozens of books, many of them on leadership. It's easy to think that if you can just read the right book, take the right class, or discover the right strategy or secret, everything will click into place.

The brutal truth is that most leaders don't actually need more knowledge in the form of a *how*. Instead, they need to find the right *who*.

The solutions are already within you. You've been solving problems your whole life, and you have what it takes to keep moving forward. But when you're stuck in leadership limbo, it's hard to see yourself clearly. A great coach can shine a light on the path that's already there.

That is precisely why the most important decision you can make isn't "What should I do next?" but "Who can help me get there faster?"

The right *who* helps you sort through the noise, challenge your assumptions, and stay accountable to your goals. Without that outside perspective, it's easy to waste years trying to figure things out on your own.

There are lots of great coaches out there, I'll admit. But if you're ready to move forward, I bring decades of experience in change management, leadership training, and hands-on coaching.

My role isn't to hand you a magic formula—it's to partner with you so you don't have to walk this road by yourself. At this point, you're a little over halfway through the book, but if you're already convinced you'd like to explore working with me, turn to page 99 for more information.

I've woven "Jeff's Leadership Tips" throughout this book so you can build momentum right now. In the rest of this chapter, I want to double down on showing you my value by offering three incredible "Leadership Boosters" that will take you even higher!

LEADERSHIP BOOSTER #1:
PICK YOUR GROWTH POINT

One of the misconceptions about leadership development is that you must work through a rigid sequence—step one, then step two, then step three. However, leadership development isn't linear. Growth happens where you need it most.

> *LEADERSHIP DEVELOPMENT ISN'T LINEAR. GROWTH HAPPENS WHERE YOU NEED IT MOST.*

That's why the SUCCESS framework is flexible. You don't have to master every element before seeing results. Instead, you can identify the areas that are holding you back and start right there.

Think of this like conducting your own personal leadership assessment. Ask yourself: *Where do I consistently get stuck?*

For example, if you can't stay calm in high-pressure situations, you will struggle to move from middle management to upper management. Why? Because leaders who lose their cool under stress send a red flag to others that they can't be trusted to handle bigger responsibilities. If this is your sticking point, focus your energy on developing calmness under pressure.

Another example: Many leaders struggle with trusting and being trustworthy. If you can't build trust—or if you can't extend it to others—you'll always face limits on how far you can lead them.

Take a quick inventory of your leadership. How many people around you do you genuinely trust? How quickly do others extend trust to you? If the answer is "not very many," the next question you want to ask yourself is: *Why is that the case?*

As we talked about in the last chapter, it's not about them. It's about *you*. You always have the ability to become more self-aware and improve your leadership.

One more example: delegation. Many leaders struggle with delegating responsibilities to others because they're afraid. They might fear losing control, being exposed, or not receiving the credit.

However, if you don't delegate effectively, you'll eventually burn out and hinder your team's growth. Start small by picking a task you would normally keep for yourself. Hand it off to someone you trust and give them space to succeed. Over time, you'll build confidence in both your leadership and your team's capabilities.

My main point is this: Don't try to tackle all the elements of SUCCESS at once. Identify one growth point, lean into it, and take deliberate steps forward. Small, focused actions are always better than giant intentions that you don't see through.

LEADERSHIP BOOSTER #2:
YOU MUST TRULY CARE

Leadership isn't about going through the motions or asking routine questions. It's far more about listening, remembering what matters, and valuing the people in front of you. It's about caring enough to follow through.

For a while, I tried to fix the issue by asking people about their families or their personal lives. The problem was, I didn't actually care. I would ask the questions, but then forget the answers. I was going through the motions of caring but didn't engage my heart.

When you focus only on results but don't care about people, you burn them—and yourself—out. Many leaders resist engaging in relationships because they don't want to be vulnerable. But a good leader understands that you can still set high standards and ask for great results, while also honoring the people who work alongside you.

LEADERSHIP BOOSTER #3:
LEARN THE DISCIPLINE OF SILENCE

One of the best leadership exercises you can do is completely counterintuitive. It doesn't involve speaking, but rather requires remaining completely silent.

The next time you are part of a meeting you're not leading, try this: Challenge yourself to listen the entire time without saying a word.

This is very difficult for leaders who are used to weighing in on every discussion. But the moment you take away the pressure to contribute, something amazing happens—you start noticing things you would otherwise miss.

You'll hear what's really being said. You'll pick up on people's tone of voice, their pauses, and their hesitation. You'll pay more attention to people's body language and the subtle power dynamics at play in the room.

Let's take it a step further. Identify one person in the group who commands attention when they speak. This is likely someone who doesn't talk often, but when they do, everyone leans in.

Study that person. Notice their timing, their composure, and how they choose their words. When you observe this, you'll start to understand the difference between the person who can't help but fill the silence with their words, versus the person who is the real influencer.

This simple act of silence builds self-control and helps you become more aware of what is happening around you. The purpose isn't to stay quiet forever. Instead, it's to learn that the less you speak and the more you listen, the more impact you will have.

OVERCOMING THE OBSTACLES

I've mentioned the opportunity to work with me directly a few times in this book. Since you're still reading, I hope you can see the value and benefit of working with a great coach.

As a way to help you think more clearly about this, I'll conclude this chapter by addressing three of the most common mental roadblocks I hear when it comes to hiring a coach.

1. *"I'm not sure it's worth the money."*

This is usually the first item that pops into people's minds when considering a coach. It's a fair question for sure because hiring a coach is an expense.

However, the real question is not about the money, but about staying stuck. How long are you willing to stay where you are? As we discussed earlier in the book, you're already paying a hefty price for staying stuck.

Consider this: Every truly successful professional has a coach (some have several). If it's good enough for Oprah Winfrey, Hugh Jackman, Eric Schmidt, and Marisa Peer, it is good enough for you!

I don't want you to look back ten or twenty years from now and wish you had taken action all those years ago. By bringing in someone who understands leadership development and has a proven model, you shorten that timeline dramatically. You avoid costly mistakes, accelerate your growth, and reap the benefits far earlier in your career.

What's that worth to you?

2. *"I don't have time for this."*

Ironically, the people who say this the most are often those who need coaching the most.

If you feel like you can't carve out an hour a week to invest in your own growth, that's a clear sign that chaos—not calm—is driving your leadership. A coach can help you learn how to slow down, get a healthier perspective, and create margin in your life.

And let's be honest: If your organization doesn't allow you to take time for development, do you really want to stay in an environment that won't let you grow?

3. *"I'm not convinced coaching will really work for me."*

As I've noted earlier, every leader's journey is unique, but the obstacles aren't. We've all wrestled with self-doubt, difficult employees, or the feeling of being passed over.

Coaching doesn't hand you generic answers—it helps you chart a faster, clearer path through your specific challenges.

But there is a hitch! You must be ready to change. In other words, you must be coachable. If you believe you already have the answers, or if you feel the problem is everyone else, you will be disappointed with the coaching experience.

That is not to say that it's all your fault; rather, it means that you are the only one you can change, so it has to be all about you—your values, thoughts, attitudes, and actions.

When you invest in yourself, you not only accelerate your career, but you also strengthen your company. Great companies are built by leaders who keep growing.

> ## GREAT COMPANIES ARE BUILT BY LEADERS WHO KEEP GROWING.

I trust this chapter has given you a lot to think about! You've learned the value of working directly with a coach, several practical tips to boost your leadership, and how to think about some of the mental obstacles many leaders face when considering hiring a coach.

Before we head into Part Three, we'll have one more stop by way of Chapter Seven. I'll show you how to take everything you've learned so far and break through the barriers that often hold leaders back.

CHAPTER SIX REFLECTION

Earlier in this chapter, I emphasized that you need a *who*, not a *how*. How have you tried to boost your leadership? By reading books, taking courses, or going to seminars and workshops? Those can all be helpful, but how would it boost your success and remove some anxiety knowing you had an experienced guide to show you the way?

BREAKING THROUGH THE BARRIERS

As we wrap up Part Two, I want to address some concerns you may have about the SUCCESS framework and how you can use it in your leadership. Let's look at each of the seven elements of the framework to identify common barriers and how to overcome them.

As I've mentioned in the book, it doesn't always require a huge, radical shift in your thinking or behavior to experience a real breakthrough.

BARRIERS TO STEADFAST CHARACTER

One of the biggest barriers to becoming more steadfast is navigating the battle between your inner critic and your inner advocate.

The critic is loud and negative. It reminds you of every mistake you've ever made and points out all the reasons you'll fail. The advocate is quieter, but it's the voice that says, "You can figure this out. You've handled tough things before, and you'll do it again."

The challenge is that most people let the critic run the show instead of strengthening their advocate.

Think of your advocate as the voice of a close friend who's someone you want to listen to. Actively search for what it's saying. Name your advocate and then ask, "What would [insert name] say about this?"

One way to become more steadfast is to practice trusting your gut. Experienced leaders look like they always know the answer, but what they've truly mastered is the ability to lean on their intuition.

You can start small. When a decision comes up, jot down your first instinct before you do all the research and analysis. Then go finish your research and check it against your gut instinct. Most of the time, you'll discover later that your initial take was correct.

Over time, that simple practice builds confidence. It teaches you that you're more capable than you think, and it helps you become the kind of leader others can rely on.

BARRIERS TO UNRELENTING TRUST

The biggest barrier to unrelenting trust is that people don't stop to think about why they don't trust someone or why someone else doesn't trust them. It just feels like this vague sense of, "Something's off." That's not very useful.

As I said earlier, Stephen M. R. Covey divides trust into two buckets: character and competence. Do you believe the person you don't quite trust is honest and has good intentions? That's character. Do you believe they actually know what they're doing? That's competence. If either one is missing, trust is shaky.

Breaking it down that way gives you something you can work with. If you feel they lack competence, they can go through training or work with a coach to improve. If your issue with them is character, you and they have a lot of deep work to do because character is the foundation of trust in any relationship.

Consider having a direct conversation with them to discuss the character gap. Be professionally honest and be prepared to hear their thoughts. Be open to changing your perspective and ask them for the same courtesy. Most issues can be resolved when you choose to have honest dialogue.

Another area where leaders get tripped up with building trust is by keeping too much emotional distance from their people. Sometimes you'll still find leaders who cling to the old-school idea that you shouldn't build relationships with employees.

But we spend most of our lives at work—why wouldn't we build genuine friendships there? The key is setting clear boundaries. Be friendly, even become close, but make sure everyone knows that when it's time to be the boss, you will be the boss.

Trust doesn't just happen. It's built intentionally, over time. And if you're not actively building it, you're already at a disadvantage as a leader.

BARRIERS TO CALM

Staying calm sounds pretty simple, doesn't it? In reality, it's one of the hardest things for leaders to practice.

The biggest barrier to calm is perspective. People convince themselves that every issue is life or death, but the world isn't going to end because you ran out of hamburgers in the middle of a lunch rush or because a report is late.

Even so, it's easy to let the small things get to you until your mind is flooded with stress and anxiety. That stress robs you of the very mental capacity you need to deal with problems effectively—and remember, feeling stressed is a choice.

Another barrier is not realizing you already know how to stay calm. Think about how you respond when your kid gets hurt. You don't panic, you move through the steps to help them. It's the same principle at work. You take one problem at a time, deal with it, and move to the next.

Staying calm doesn't mean you don't have emotions.

> TRUE CALM IS ABOUT KEEPING PERSPECTIVE AND REFUSING TO LET CHAOS CONTROL YOU.

BARRIERS TO COLLABORATION AND DELEGATION

The barrier most leaders face here is relationships. Some folks, especially those with a technical or engineering mindset, don't see the point in building them. They'll say, "I'll connect with someone if I need something from them, but why waste time on small talk if I don't?"

The problem is, if you show up only when you need something, people notice. The relationship starts to feel transactional instead of collaborative, and over time you lose trust and influence.

Picture your relationships in three tiers.

At the top are your closest friends—the tiny handful of people you'd rush to help at a moment's notice. At the bottom are acquaintances—people you've met but don't really know. In the middle are colleagues and peers you interact with all the time. And it's in that middle group where collaboration lives.

You don't have to be best friends, but you do need enough connection to build trust, swap favors, and move projects forward without everything turning into a big negotiation.

As I noted in an earlier chapter, delegation is another sticking point. Many leaders struggle to let go, thinking they need to be in the weeds to keep control. But if you're doing the work that should belong to your team, something's broken.

Collaboration and delegation go hand in hand—you extend your power by building trust and then letting others run with the tasks at hand.

BARRIERS TO EXECUTIVE PRESENCE

Executive presence is one of those things that's hard to define but easy to spot. When someone walks into a room and instantly commands respect, that's executive presence.

The challenge for most leaders is that they believe it's about charisma or having the right title. But it's mostly about emotional intelligence and listening.

Two primary barriers often prevent people from fully developing their executive presence.

The first is emotions. As a leader, your emotions can't be in the driver's seat. If you lose control, your team loses confidence. Emotional intelligence is simply learning to manage those emotions instead of letting them manage you. But being stoic is equally unnerving to your team, so remember to show a balanced persona. Don't let your emotions take over, but be sure your team knows that you are human.

The second barrier is the need to prove you're the smartest person in the room. That may have worked when you were climbing the corporate ladder, but at higher levels, everyone around you is just as sharp.

That's the real foundation of executive presence: calm authority, emotional control, and the discipline to listen more than you speak.

The leaders who stand out are the ones who know when to stay quiet, when to listen, and when to speak with precision.

> THE LEADERS WHO STAND OUT ARE THE ONES WHO KNOW WHEN TO STAY QUIET, WHEN TO LISTEN, AND WHEN TO SPEAK WITH PRECISION.

BARRIERS TO SAVVY BUSINESS ACUMEN

When it comes to the savvy business acumen element of SUCCESS, the biggest obstacle is thinking in silos. Leaders often get so locked into their own department or area of expertise that they forget the rest of the company even exists.

Finance people obsess over their spreadsheets without realizing how their policies choke the workflow in operations, or IT rolls out a system that makes life easier for them but creates headaches for everybody else.

These leaders might be focused deep in their lane, but they've lost the broader perspective of how the whole organization fits together.

That's why I use the word *savvy* instead of just *business acumen*. Acumen is knowledge, but savvy adds shrewdness—an ability to see how the puzzle pieces connect.

Without a sense of savvy, you'll always be making short-sighted calls. Leaders who lack savvy end up stuck at the tactical level. They can't participate meaningfully in strategic planning. And if you can't think strategically, you're not really leading.

BARRIERS TO SELF-DEVELOPMENT

The hardest part of self-development is seeing yourself clearly. Many people simply don't take time to look in a mirror. If you've never built that habit, you either skip self-reflection altogether or you go with the shallow version: "How'd I do today? Fine."

That approach doesn't move the needle in your self-development.

What helps the most is critical self-reflection. It means going a layer deeper without beating yourself up. After a meeting or a tough one-on-one, ask: *What actually happened? What did I do that helped? What made it worse? If I had a do-over, what would I try?*

This isn't fuel for your inner critic; it's simply planning for next time.

You don't need to turn this into a big ordeal. Two or three minutes right after the moment is usually enough. If an interaction went well, capture *why* so you can repeat it. If it went sideways, try to name the specific thing that made it unsafe or confusing for the other person.

This one insight is often all you need to improve.

JEFF'S LEADERSHIP TIP #4:
STEP OUTSIDE OF YOUR BUBBLE

One of the very best ways to become a savvier and more effective leader is to get outside of the "leadership bubble" you exist in every day.

If you know only the people in your department, you will tend to make decisions that cause ripple effects elsewhere in the company. You can avoid that trap by deliberately learning how other parts of the business work.

Here's an easy, practical step: Go have lunch with someone from a different department. Ask them about what they do, how their team is structured, and what challenges they're facing.

If you're in a remote work situation and lunch isn't possible, join a meeting ten minutes early and strike up a conversation with whoever shows up. Simple questions like "What projects are you working on?" or "What's the hardest part of your team's job right now?" can open lots of doors. If others are not available before a meeting, consider setting up a separate call to ask them for more detail about something you hear during the meeting. Be resilient with your learning.

When you get outside of your bubble, you will build stronger relationships and no longer be just an email address to the people outside your area. You also build your knowledge of other parts of the business, which translates into insights and awareness that separates the leaders who will go further, faster.

Every new conversation you have adds another piece to the puzzle, making you a more well-rounded and credible leader.

That concludes Part Two of this book. Congrats! We are well over halfway there! But the even better news is that your new and improved leadership journey is only beginning.

In Part Three, I will challenge you with the key question: "Are you ready for SUCCESS?" I hope the answer is a firm *yes* as we explore a few stories and ideas for how you can put SUCCESS into practice, and a vision for a new, more confident you.

CHAPTER SEVEN REFLECTION

Sometimes in life and leadership, you don't break through barriers because you're simply not ready. You may have the skills, connections, and resources—but nothing will happen until you decide to act on what you've read.

Answer this question honestly: Do you feel ready to break through the barriers I've listed in this chapter and grow into the leader you know you can be?

Having thought about that question, what is your inner advocate saying right now?

PART THREE

ARE YOU READY FOR SUCCESS?

STORIES OF SUCCESS

It's one thing to hear me talk about the SUCCESS framework and how it can help you. But it's another to see it lived out in people's lives.

In this chapter, I'll show you what can happen when leaders put these ideas to work. I've included three different stories.

The first one focuses on one leader's personal transformation when he stepped into a much bigger role than anything he had taken on before. The second one is a bigger-picture case study that answers the question, "What happens to whole groups of leaders when they misunderstand what leadership really is?" And the third is a composite story based on lots of people I've worked with over the years—they were stuck and overwhelmed, but one small change made the difference.

All of these stories show what can happen when you truly commit to grow as a leader. Near the end of the chapter, I'll offer some concluding thoughts about the power of transformation in your leadership.

THE PLANT MANAGER WHO NEEDED TO LET GO

One of my coaching clients had spent almost thirty years running a small facility with about fifty employees. He was the type of leader who loved to roll up his sleeves and do the work himself.

If he needed a chart, he drew it. If something broke, he fixed it. That all worked fine in a small setting, but everything changed when he was promoted to lead a facility with 1,500 employees.

The problem was simple: His old way of working could not scale to the new location. If he kept trying to do everything by himself, he was going to burn out fast and drag the whole operation down with him.

That is where the value of coaching came in. We worked together over several months to address several key areas:

- Trust: He needed to learn to trust his people.

- Delegation: He needed to learn how to let go of work that wasn't his.

- Calm: He needed to learn how to silence his inner critic who was telling him he wasn't ready to take on the challenge.

As you can imagine, it wasn't easy. However, he grew tremendously during this period. In fact, this leader wrote me a letter soon after he made the transition, saying that he believed our work together set the stage for his success.

He learned how to be intentional about building trust, how to delegate with purpose, and how to keep steady in a much more chaotic and much bigger environment than what he'd been used to. Most leaders would have crumbled making such a big move, but he was able to do it successfully with the help of great coaching.

That's the story of one individual. But let's zoom out a bit and see what happens when entire categories of leaders need help adjusting to new roles.

LEADERS WHO EXPERIENCE A SURPRISING CAREER CHANGE

Most people believe that moving up the ladder is just doing the same job with more responsibility. But that's not true. When you go from being an individual contributor to a manager, or from a manager to a director, you're not just being promoted—you are completely changing careers.

This change in role and responsibilities is profound, and usually catches people off guard.

For example, the best engineer suddenly finds himself leading people instead of solving problems. Or the new VP discovers that her main job is sitting in meetings, shaping strategy, and speaking in the language of dollars rather than the project-oriented work she is used to.

When this shift happens, it feels like their head is in the clouds because it's completely different than what they were expecting. The new role is not just their old job with a few things tacked on. It's something completely new and different.

I have worked with dozens of leaders who didn't see this massive change coming. They struggled because they were still acting like practitioners and "doers" instead of leaders. Through this method, I have helped them understand the difference between tactical and strategic work. They came to understand that every step up requires changing focus to a new set of details. The higher you go, the more you focus on guiding the company.

As a result, these leaders stopped resenting meetings and started seeing them as the real work of leadership. They were able to understand how quality and efficiency translate into actual profit for the business. And they were also able to let go of their old identity and step into a new, more powerful persona.

When leaders see promotions as a career change instead of just "something extra," it opens up a whole new perspective.

But what about the leaders who never make it that far—the ones who feel stuck and ready to walk away from it all?

YOUR LEADERSHIP MAKEOVER

People enter the SUCCESS framework because they feel out of sync and can't pinpoint why. Or perhaps they know there is a higher level of leadership that they want to reach. They might have the title, the office, maybe even the big paycheck, but they feel unsettled inside.

Some of the signs I've seen many times include:

- They second-guess themselves.
- They avoid delegating because it feels easier to do things themselves.
- They get flustered in meetings.
- They are too rigid with their teams.
- They lean into workplace politics so hard that nobody quite trusts them.
- They just can't get the results they expect.

People notice these signs because you can only fake it for so long. You can't fake calm, trust, authenticity, and real leadership. When you don't have these qualities nailed down, it shows. The people you lead pick up on it instantly.

That's the "before" picture. The "after" picture is almost like a leadership makeover. But it's not just a surface-level polish. We're talking a deep, meaningful, personal change that shows genuine transformation. People can see it and feel it.

When leaders go through this process, these are some of the typical results:

They become calmer and less chaotic. Their teams see that they are not reacting with panic anymore, but are handling pressure and bringing emotional stability.

They build trust as the new foundation of their leadership. They start showing up more authentically, their teams run more smoothly, and people feel safer with them—all resulting in better performance from everyone.

They become better at delegation. They no longer try to do everything themselves but trust others with more responsibilities. Work is done faster, and the leader has more time for strategic thinking and people development.

They become more confident. The leader no longer walks into a room and wonders if they belong there. They make better decisions and can explain those decisions with confidence, even when others disagree.

They feel more balanced. Instead of feeling burned out all the time, they have more energy and joy, which translates into showing up with more capacity for important conversations.

Keep in mind, none of this is magic. And it's not just reserved for people who are so-called born leaders. These are skills anyone can learn or strengthen. With the right coaching and framework, anybody can grow their leadership muscles.

When this happens, your teams become more engaged, more work gets done, you see better results all around, and you're having fun again! You will also be promoted more quickly because your company sees you contributing in a way you haven't before.

I hope that reading these stories and seeing the possibilities has you more excited than ever about your potential leadership transformation! In the next chapter, we'll dive even deeper as I share a few principles for putting this framework into practice.

CHAPTER EIGHT RELFECTION

In this chapter, you've read three different stories:

- The plant manager who had to let go

- Leaders who needed to understand that promotions involve a career change

- Stuck leaders who needed to stay calm and build connections

Where do you see yourself in these stories? Your situation may be different, but I'll bet you can relate to at least some of the details. Can you envision yourself undergoing a similar leadership transformation? What might that look like specifically?

PUTTING SUCCESS INTO PRACTICE

Do you remember that feeling of being in school, sitting in class, feeling bored to death as the teacher droned on, wondering, *What does any of this have to do with my real life?*

I've had that same experience many times. And not just as a student in school, but as a learner when it comes to leadership principles. Countless times, I've been reading a book or attending a seminar or workshop, and thought to myself, *What does this have to do with real leadership?*

As a man who's been in leadership roles most of my professional life, I know the difference between principles that work … and principles that don't.

I designed the SUCCESS framework, first and foremost, to be a system that *works for you*. But I don't just want to make that assertion and hope you blindly believe it. Instead, I want to show you in this chapter how to apply SUCCESS in the real rough-and-tumble world of leadership—how to take it a step further, and why coaching is the ideal way to ensure strong, lasting results.

SUCCESS APPLIES TO YOUR ENTIRE WORLD

Many people believe that leadership only kicks in when you get a title such as *manager, director,* or *VP*. But the reality is that you're leading all the time.

Leadership is simply having influence over others. And the more confident you are, the more influence you have. Your influence shows up everywhere: at work, at home, in your community, even in the way you show up for your friends.

That's why the SUCCESS framework doesn't just apply to your life on the job. It applies to the whole person. You don't get to leave home at home and work at work. If you're struggling with something in your personal life, that baggage walks into the office with you.

Likewise, if you're having a brutal day at work, your family is going to feel it when you get home. You carry it all with you, all the time. Try as you might, it's nearly impossible to shut it off. This means if you get better in one area, you start to see the ripple effects everywhere else in your life.

So, when you think about applying the SUCCESS framework, don't limit it to just your career. Use it in your home, with your peers, in your community, and especially in your own self-talk.

Leadership is for the *whole person*. The sooner you connect those dots, the sooner you'll stop compartmentalizing and start seeing real growth in every corner of your life.

THREE STEPS TO TAKE IT FURTHER

The temptation with a book like this is to read it, nod your head, maybe underline or highlight some sentences or paragraphs … and then put it back on the shelf. Nothing changes, and you stay stuck.

Except now, you're even more frustrated because you know what you should be doing and never did.

If you want the concepts in this book to make a real difference in your life, it has to move from interesting ideas to your actual to-do list. That is where real, honest transformation can happen. Let me give you three simple steps.

First, decide what part of the SUCCESS framework you need to focus on right now. Don't try to master everything at once. Maybe it's staying calm under pressure. Maybe it's building trust. Maybe it's learning how to delegate.

Pick one, and write down what you're going to do about it this week. Don't wait until someday. Do it this week.

Second, make yourself accountable. Sure, it's hard to hold yourself accountable. Life gets busy, a crisis or two happens, and your old habits creep back in. That's why you need another person in the mix.

Find a friend, a coworker, your spouse—someone who has enough influence in your life that when they call you out, you'll actually listen. Be sure to give them permission to challenge you and thank them when they do!

Third, be radically honest with yourself about whether you're ready for change. It's hard to get out of your comfort zone. Of course, some people will read this and jump in right away. But most others will need a few weeks before they finally commit.

That's okay. What matters is deciding at some point that you're not content with "good enough." You're finally ready to say goodbye to the past and welcome your new and exciting future.

Don't just close this book and walk away. Pick your focus, put it on your calendar, get someone to hold you accountable, and start moving. That's how you turn information into transformation.

MAKING YOUR BIG DECISION

I talk to so many leaders who are smart, capable, and driven, but they keep hitting closed windows and don't know why. A good coach removes years of trial and error and gives you insight into what's holding you back.

That's exactly where I come in.

It's no exaggeration to say that I live and breathe leadership. I've spent my whole career inside organizations, watching what works and what doesn't, and helping leaders grow. When we work together, my job isn't to give you a cookie-cutter answer or judge your decisions. It's to step back and help you see the bigger picture from a broader vantage point.

What's happening inside you? What's going on in your environment? What's holding you back? Those are the kinds of questions, in addition to many others, we explore in coaching.

And honestly, most of the time—nine times out of ten—the missing piece is internal. It's usually not an outside person or situation holding you back. It's something within you. The great news? You can change *that* anytime. But it's hard to do this on your own. That's why a great coach is so critical.

One of the reasons my coaching works is that I provide a completely safe space. People can tell me anything. I don't share what one client says with another client. I don't run to your boss with a summary of our sessions. If you don't feel safe, it's pretty hard for you to grow.

If you're reading this and wondering whether coaching is worth the time and monetary investment, think of it this way: You can keep trying to figure it out alone and maybe get there in ten or fifteen years—or you can get an outside perspective from someone who spends every day helping leaders grow *and get there in a few months.*

You'll move faster, avoid a lot of pain, and finally see what's been in your blind spot all along.

Think about how valuable it will be to shorten your time to success, avoid costly mistakes, and accelerate your career.

Before moving on to our final chapter, let's look at one more leadership tip you can begin implementing immediately, whatever your situation.

JEFF'S LEADERSHIP TIP #5:
LEADING WITH CALM IN TIMES OF CHAOS

To some degree or another, chaos always exists. I define chaos as "a lack of orderly flow." The breadth and depth of the chaos around us doesn't usually reach the level of a global crisis, but obviously, it's possible.

As a leader, you not only have to deal with your own chaos, but also that of your team. Some days, this is reasonably easy. But other days, it would be easier to fly a kite through a hurricane.

We are living through a time of great cultural, economic, and social upheaval. This isn't the first time this has happened, and it won't be the last. Now more than ever, your team is looking to you for support, confidence, guidance, empathy, and hope.

How do you shoulder all of this and support them without losing your mind? Let me suggest two strategies.

First, one of the most important leadership skills you can learn is how to keep your mind calm. When you're not calm, it's usually because you have so many things coming at you that it puts your brain into a state of panic.

You don't have all of the answers. No one does. You just have to learn how to keep your brain out of panic mode.

Remember, no matter what the situation is, you can only start from where you are and move forward. Leaders, especially those new to leadership, panic because they are trying to solve everything at once, but their brains can only complete one task at a time. When you start feeling overwhelmed, take a deep breath and focus on staying calm.

Second, learn to develop more empathy. Your team members are all facing a different set of challenges. As a leader, you need to understand their perspective and go where they are (mentally) so you can help them. It doesn't mean you take their baggage for them, it means you understand what they are carrying and you show compassion for their situation.

Empathy is your ability to recognize and understand (possibly even appreciate) the thoughts and feelings of others. This doesn't mean you have to agree with them; it simply means you understand where they're coming from. Being empathetic requires the ability to manage your emotions well enough that you can set them aside when you are considering another person's point of view.

By sidelining your own emotions, you will be able to see their emotions and thoughts. Once you are able to look at their point of view from a more neutral perspective, you can ask questions that will help you understand them more deeply. The objective is to understand them well enough that both of you can find common ground to work through any problem together.

Improving your empathy starts with listening more to other people. A simple exercise you can do with a friend or colleague is to ask them how they feel about a given topic. Start with a simple topic and just have a conversation about it. At the end of the conversation, describe how you think the person thinks and feels about this topic. Let them tell you how close your description is to their true thoughts and feelings. The gap between your description and theirs indicates your skill at being empathetic.

While you are opening up to understand them, be willing to show them who you are and what you are facing also. People are more trusting when you're willing to show your vulnerabilities. This doesn't mean you have to share personal or embarrassing information. It just means letting them know you're human, you face challenges too, and you're still showing up where you're needed.

Now more than ever is the time for you to hone your leadership skills so you can be the calm, empathetic leader others want to follow.

That's ultimately what this whole book has been about—giving you the tools and resources to be as effective a leader as possible. In our final chapter, I'll take everything we've been talking about so far and give you a vision of what this can look like in action.

CHAPTER NINE REFLECTION

For this action step, I'll keep it brief and straightforward with a single question: What is the most significant barrier preventing you from moving forward with a leadership coach—and what if that barrier could be eliminated?

INTRODUCING THE NEW, CONFIDENT YOU

We've come a long way in *Leadership SUCCESS*! Even though this book is short, I've done my best to pack it full of practical insights and a clear line of sight to where you want to go as a leader.

Let's do a quick review:

In Part One, we spent some time thinking about the missing ingredient of leadership: confidence. When leaders lack confidence, they become stuck in leadership limbo. This is why you can benefit from a great coach who can help you get unstuck and headed in the right direction.

In Part Two, we explored my SUCCESS framework. I detailed how these elements can help you level up your leadership, understand how they can apply to your situation, and accelerate it even further.

Then in Part Three, I shared stories of SUCCESS to help you see how this framework can work in different situations.

You learned how to put it into practice with a few more tips so that you can become a new, bolder version of yourself as a leader.

All of this has been in service of empowering you to become a *new, confident you*. With that in mind, in this chapter, I'll share a few brief thoughts on how to accelerate your journey to becoming a greater leader. I'll also expand on the ROI of investing in yourself and detail a few pathways to working together.

ACCELERATING YOUR LEADERSHIP JOURNEY

Almost anybody can learn *some* leadership skills if they stay in their current position long enough. It's why you often see people getting management, director, or VP roles in their fifties or sixties. Most of the time, those people didn't have a pathway to success or intentionally pursue that goal. They just stuck around long enough to outlast everybody.

I don't want you to ever get a promotion or to have success of any kind because you were the default choice. I want you to have success because you were intentional, you earned it, and you had your eyes on the prize until you reached your goal!

If you resonate with that, you probably don't want to wait for years or even decades to see results. You can start enjoying more success right away.

The value of great coaching is that it can help you do just that. Earlier in the book I used the phrase "closed window" to describe the feeling of being able to see where you want to go, but still being frustrated because you can't seem to get it open. Coaching helps you *open the closed window*.

Instead of stumbling through mistakes for the next twenty years, you get clarity in six months. Instead of waiting until you're burned out and overwhelmed with stress because you haven't learned to delegate, you can begin mastering that today and free up your energy for higher-level work.

It's the difference between walking and flying. You *could* reach the other side of the country on foot in a few months… or you could arrive in a matter of hours by plane. Coaching is the airplane that will take you further, faster, and higher.

Even if you feel like you already know most of this stuff, I promise you this: There is always another level. To paraphrase leadership expert Kevin Cashman: We're authentic to what we know today, but that means we're inauthentic to what we'll learn tomorrow.

In other words, growth never stops. Coaching helps you step into tomorrow's version of yourself today.

The choice is simple. You can learn leadership the hard way, over decades of trial and error. Or you can fast-track your growth by working with somebody who has already been down that road and can help you navigate around the obstacles.

THE ROI OF COACHING

We've touched on this topic in the book already, but let me dive a bit deeper here.

The elephant in the room when it comes to coaching is always the cost. If you hire a coach, it's an investment. You are probably wondering if it's worth it.

I look at it this way: Leadership coaching isn't a cost. It's an *investment that gives you leverage.* You're putting in time and money to multiply something much bigger—your influence, your career trajectory, your income, and your peace of mind.

Think about what happens when you don't invest in yourself:

• You stay stuck at the same level.

- You keep second-guessing yourself in meetings.
- You keep avoiding delegation because it feels easier to do it yourself.
- You feel anxious because you're not sure your team fully trusts you.

What is the result of all this? Every day that passes, opportunities slip by because you weren't quite ready. One of the most defeating conversations I've had is being told I wasn't quite ready after interviewing for my dream job.

Now compare that with the upside:

- What is it worth to get promoted faster because your company sees you stepping up in a new way?
- What is it worth to have a team that runs smoother, delivers better results, and gives you back your evenings with your family?
- What is it worth to show up calm and confident instead of anxious and reactive?

That's the ROI of coaching. You're not paying for information—you're buying acceleration, transformation, and results. The reality is, the people who get to the top aren't just the smartest or the hardest working. They're the ones who invested in themselves early and often.

When you think about the cost of coaching, don't say to yourself, *What does this take away from me?* Instead, ask yourself: *What will this investment unlock for me that I can't unlock on my own?*

PATHWAYS TO THE NEW YOU

Let's explore a few pathways to a new, improved, more confident you. I know that's the leader you can become! These are the ways we can work together, depending on your needs:

Online training: I offer self-directed training you can complete at your own pace that includes limited access directly to me for answers to your questions.

1:1 Coaching: This is the most personal option, and the one I do the most. We work together directly for a specific length of time. This type of coaching is where real breakthroughs occur because I tailor it to your specific situation, goals, and challenges.

Workshops: For a deeper dive into the principles I've laid out in *Leadership SUCCESS,* I offer customized training where leaders roll up their sleeves, deal with real-world problems, and come away with actionable strategies.

Whatever pathway you choose, the most important thing is to *act.* Although I hope you've enjoyed this book, the worst thing you can do right now is put it on the shelf and go back to business as usual.

I challenge you to decide today what version of yourself you want to become. Do you want to be the leader who is stuck, always reacting to the fires around you, or the one who overcomes and rises above challenges, inspiring others in the process?

The next move you make doesn't need to be big or dramatic. It can be as easy as reaching out to schedule a workshop or booking a coaching call. Or it might be as simple as applying something you've learned and putting it into practice next week.

The point is to do something to accelerate your leadership success. Why? Because the "new you" doesn't have to be a vague, undefined vision you keep for the future. The new you begins to emerge the moment you decide to move forward.

CHAPTER TEN REFLECTION

For this final reflection, I challenge you to take five minutes to imagine what your life could be like one year from now.

Picture yourself walking into a meeting with confidence, delegating important tasks with clarity and trust, and leading with calm authority. Imagine what it would feel like to know that your team trusts you more, your boss sees you as ready for the next promotion, and your family sees a newfound energy in you.

Now ask yourself: *What is holding me back from making the one decision that can move me forward toward that goal?* Write it down and commit to doing it. Your future self will thank you!

YOUR SUCCESS STARTS NOW

A number of years ago, I heard a story about a hiker named Aron Ralston, who was literally stuck between a rock and a hard place.

He was out hiking alone in a canyon when a large rock fell on his arm, wedging it into place. For many hours, he did everything he could to try to extract himself from the situation, just like anyone would.

Finally, he had to resort to the unthinkable. Mustering all of his courage and strength, he had to break his own arm and saw through his muscles, tendons, and skin to free himself. He literally cut off his own arm to save his life.

It's a pretty gruesome image, isn't it? Yet it's not entirely unlike the situation many leaders find themselves in. They may not be like that young man who faced a literal life-or-death situation. However, when they consider the stakes they face in their leadership, it literally feels like they are caught between *a rock and a hard place.*

They're immobilized and unable to move. These leaders can't go backwards because that feels unthinkable. Yet they can't move forward, either.

As I noted back in Chapter One, these leaders are stuck in limbo.

I've written *Leadership SUCCESS* to help leaders just like them—and just like you—to get unstuck and moving in the right direction.

YOUR FUTURE SELF THANKS YOU

As we wrap up this book, I want to challenge you with a quick exercise. It won't take long, but I promise it's incredibly powerful.

Take a few moments to imagine yourself at a retirement party. It may be a few years from now, or even decades into the future. Regardless of the time frame, visualize yourself sitting near the stage. One by one, people who worked with you come to the microphone and share stories of how you changed their lives.

- What kinds of stories would they tell?

- How might they describe the ways you changed them?

- In what ways were their lives and families richer because of your influence?

- How did you help your company grow and succeed, enabling it to serve its customers better?

It's a powerful picture, isn't it?

Just think, that picture doesn't have to live only in your imagination. It can exist in reality, no matter the specific time frame. All it takes is one simple decision to transform your future by working with a great coach.

That's why I invite you to take the next step in working with me. Let me share specifically a few ways we can work together:

Email me directly at: jeff@foundations4.com

Please scan the QR code below to visit https://foundations4leadership.com for:

- Online training opportunities

- Details of coaching packages

- Details about speaking engagements and workshops

WOULD YOU REVIEW THIS BOOK?

If you enjoyed reading this book, would you kindly take a few moments to leave a review wherever you purchased it (and perhaps even Goodreads.com)?

I'm grateful for your support. Thank you!

GRATITUDE

Jennie, thank you for stepping into the middle of this adventure and supporting a dream that was still finding its footing. The best is yet to come, sweetheart.

Kristine Ayuzawa, you partnered with me as I learned what it truly meant to be a coach, and you've stayed present—even from half a world away—through the whole adventure. I cherish your friendship and support.

Raj Anderson, your friendship, guidance, and moral support mean a lot and are certainly part of my success story.

For someone who hasn't been there before, transforming a bunch of noisy thoughts into a book is a fascinatingly frustrating process. Honorée Corder, thank you for lighting the path and bringing the best of the best team who made it seem easy. Kent Sanders, M. J. James, Mike McConnell, and Dino Marino, you are all wonderful and have my deepest gratitude.

To all the folks I've been fortunate to coach. Each one of you contributed by giving back as much as you were given. This book wouldn't exist if you hadn't shared part of your journey with me.

ABOUT THE AUTHOR

Jeff Robinson brings over 25 years of experience in leadership as a trainer, mentor, and coach. Practical, efficient, and easy-going, he has a gift for helping people stay calm in the midst of challenges. Jeff is passionate about developing self-awareness in others and guiding them to grow into individuals that colleagues admire and want to follow.

He earned a Master's in Organizational Leadership from Norwich University and is a Professional Certified Coach (ICF). Over the years, Jeff has worked with professionals in healthcare, finance, technology, manufacturing, the military, and more. From new supervisors to senior executives, he equips people with the tools to navigate culture, succeed in their roles, and reach their full potential.

When not working with clients, Jeff enjoys woodworking, reading fantasy/science fiction, riding motorcycles, and spending time outdoors with his family and dogs. Find out more at Foundations4Leadership.com.

Poem – 01
God Knows Your End

Working out is challenging sometimes
It's a breeze once you get used to the routine
You work out with ease
I keep tissue handy just in case I sneeze
Life challenges can bring you to your knees
I hear early morning chirping from the birds
And buzzing from the bees
While I listen to the wind whistle through the trees

The sun shines bright and Jesus is always the light
To worship him is a delight
And I know he has me in his sight
I don't have to worry from morning to night

'Cause as long as I got Jesus I know I'm alright
The storm comes and may give you a fright
But God says fear not I will take you to a higher height
Where you can be in peace and everything is as still as night

Trials come to make you strong
You might feel alone
But as time goes by you will see
How God carried you all along
And how he sees you as more precious than a jewel
That he won't let get crushed by a stone
God wants you to choose him
So he can welcome you home
Into eternal life known as paradise
Where the father, Jesus, and your family have waited for you
Even old friends who you once knew
And others who made it in that left you on earth with a clue
About all that Jesus had in store for you
But while you are still on the earth
Pray continuously and do your best to live right before him
Always keep a repentant and a forgiving heart
Stay free from sin and don't let your relationship with God grow apart
God knows we will fall
The word says a righteous man falls seven times but rises again
Stay repentive to God he knows your heart and he knows your end.

POEM – 02
THE STRENGTH I GAINED

The fresh smell of the summer breeze
Is the reason why in Jesus I believe
No one can take away my pain
And let the sun shine when it rains
Like when the Presence of Jesus came
And by God's grace I was able to maintain
Jesus' strength is how I overcame
What causes me to go insane
The frustration in my brain
That causes my thinking to strain
The moment I give it to Jesus to take away the pain
The frustration leaves as quick as it came
Still, I remain changed
'Cause nobody experiences Jesus and remains the same
Thoughts of "I can't make it" and looking back on how far
I came
The devil is a liar 'cause I elevated through all the
strength I gained.

HE WILL GIVE ME REST

The leaves look beautiful falling off of the trees
In the springtime, just looking at the view
Of the leaves all around the tree
Makes my creativity expand to all it can be
The future is hard to see
But I still see success as I imagine

Me walking in the life that God has for me
I walk with joy, peace, and tranquility
God directs my path as I move in mobility
God delivered me from my old mentality
As he separated me from the world
To a Christ-like reality
This day I am working on my success
Through all I've been through
God was just putting me to the test

All my sins I already confess
God knows when and where to bless
Because he already has my address
I've got to keep going, God showed me how to press
So in the end, he will give me rest.

Poem - 04
ONLY GOD CAN STRENGTHEN YOU THROUGH THE STORM

Life can be frustrating when you are going through a storm
Trying to figure out who is for you and who is not
Leaving your heart in a mixture of cold and warm
Trying to figure it out yourself will be the norm
But sometimes your way leaves your heart torn
'Cause only God can strengthen you through the storm.

I HAVE JESUS IN THE FIGHT

I pray day and night
I got spiritual appetite
On my journey in this fight
I can't lose sight
When life goes wrong
Only Jesus makes it right,
I am a winner
Because I have Jesus in the
fight.

Poem – 06
GOD LOVES HIS PEOPLE

Smiling at my future and it's smiling back
The devil thought he had me when he came to attack
God cut him off and put me further on track
God's spirit never left, no need to ask
When he will be back
He gives me power to get wealth
So for money, I won't lack
I feel God's presence in the atmosphere so strong
That the devil can't hack
God protects me and pushes the devil back
And God loves his people, and that's a matter of fact.

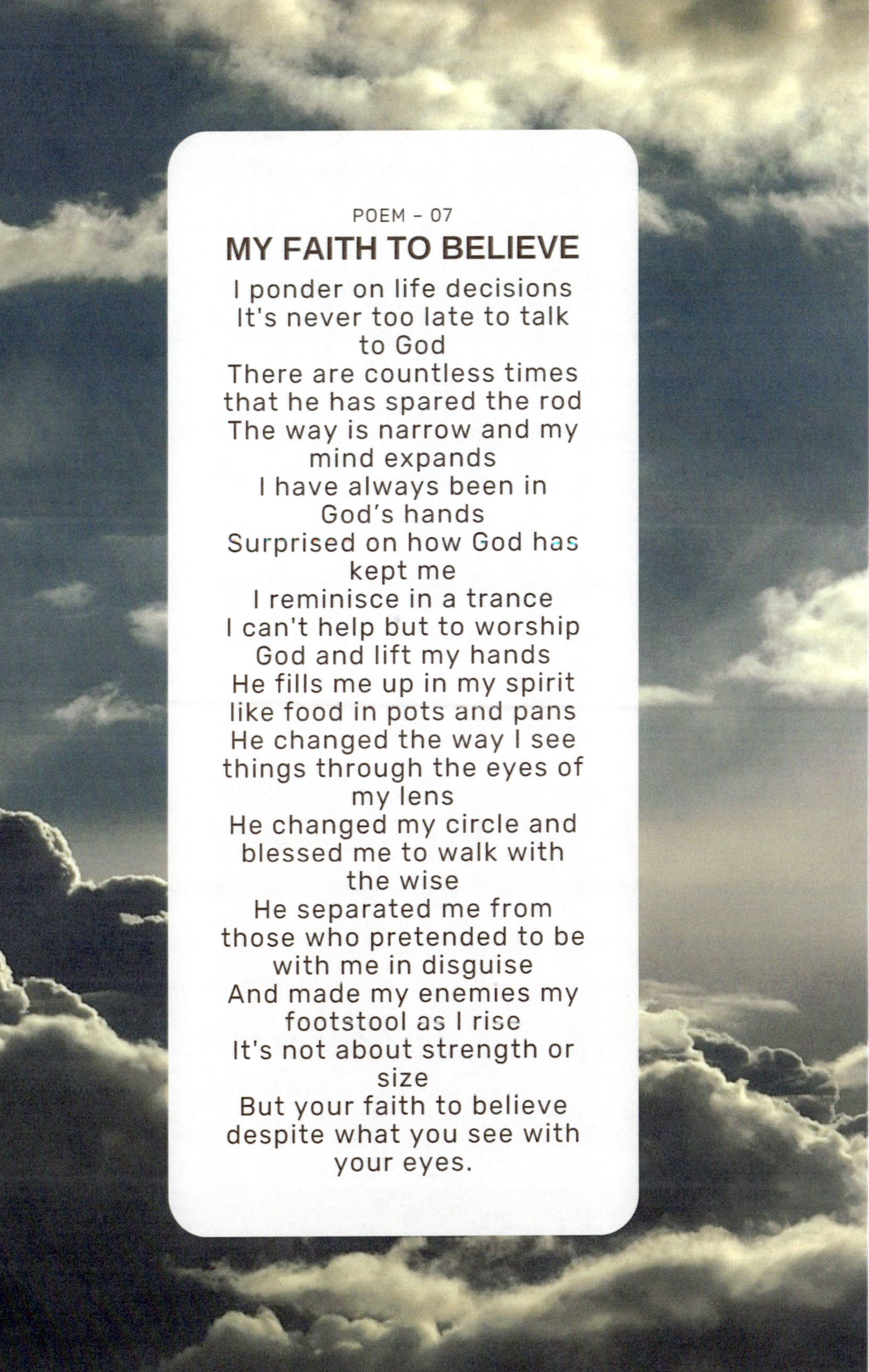

POEM – 07

MY FAITH TO BELIEVE

I ponder on life decisions
It's never too late to talk
to God
There are countless times
that he has spared the rod
The way is narrow and my
mind expands
I have always been in
God's hands
Surprised on how God has
kept me
I reminisce in a trance
I can't help but to worship
God and lift my hands
He fills me up in my spirit
like food in pots and pans
He changed the way I see
things through the eyes of
my lens
He changed my circle and
blessed me to walk with
the wise
He separated me from
those who pretended to be
with me in disguise
And made my enemies my
footstool as I rise
It's not about strength or
size
But your faith to believe
despite what you see with
your eyes.

WELCOME US HOME

I LIVE LIFE FREE, MY FAITH IS AS TALL AS AN OAK TREE
SEARCHING FOR SOMETHING SWEET GOT ME BUZZING
LIKE A HONEY BEE
GOD'S PRESENCE IS SWEETER THAN HONEY AND
DEEPER THAN THE OCEAN SEA
GOD MADE LIFE FOR US TO LIVE ABUNDANTLY
I SPEAK FROM THE HEART BUT NOT TOO EMOTIONALLY
I STAND STRONG BUT I AM NEVER STANDING ALONE
GOD HAS THE ANSWER MORE INFORMATIVE THAN
GOOGLE CHROME
HIS LIGHT IS BRIGHTER THAN FIRE TO A STONE
HE HEALS MY BODY AND STRENGTHENS MY BONE
HE IS A GOD LIKE NO OTHER THAT CAN'T BE CLONED
THIS LIFE IS A SHORT TIME
ONE DAY WE'RE HERE THEN YEARS LATER WE'RE GONE
WE SING FAREWELLS AND SAY SO LONG
WE ARE NOT FAR GONE 'CAUSE THE FATHER IS ON THE
THRONE
TO SAY WELL DONE AND WELCOME US HOME.

POEM – 08
GOD KEPT ME

God never left me neglected
He saved my soul from the devil, he intercepted
Even when I didn't expect it
God made sure I wasn't too affected
For this calling, God had me elected
I accepted everything God suggested
The word says whatever concerns me God will
perfect it
I got to keep stepping, daily prayer be my weapon
God keeps me when I weep
He lifts me to my feet
He changed my words of speech
He delivered me from the leech, that's the devil we
discreet
When I pray, God comes to the meet and greet
I let God take the wheel and I just have a seat
God is always on point, he never misses a beat
Jesus is king, he created the grain and the wheat.

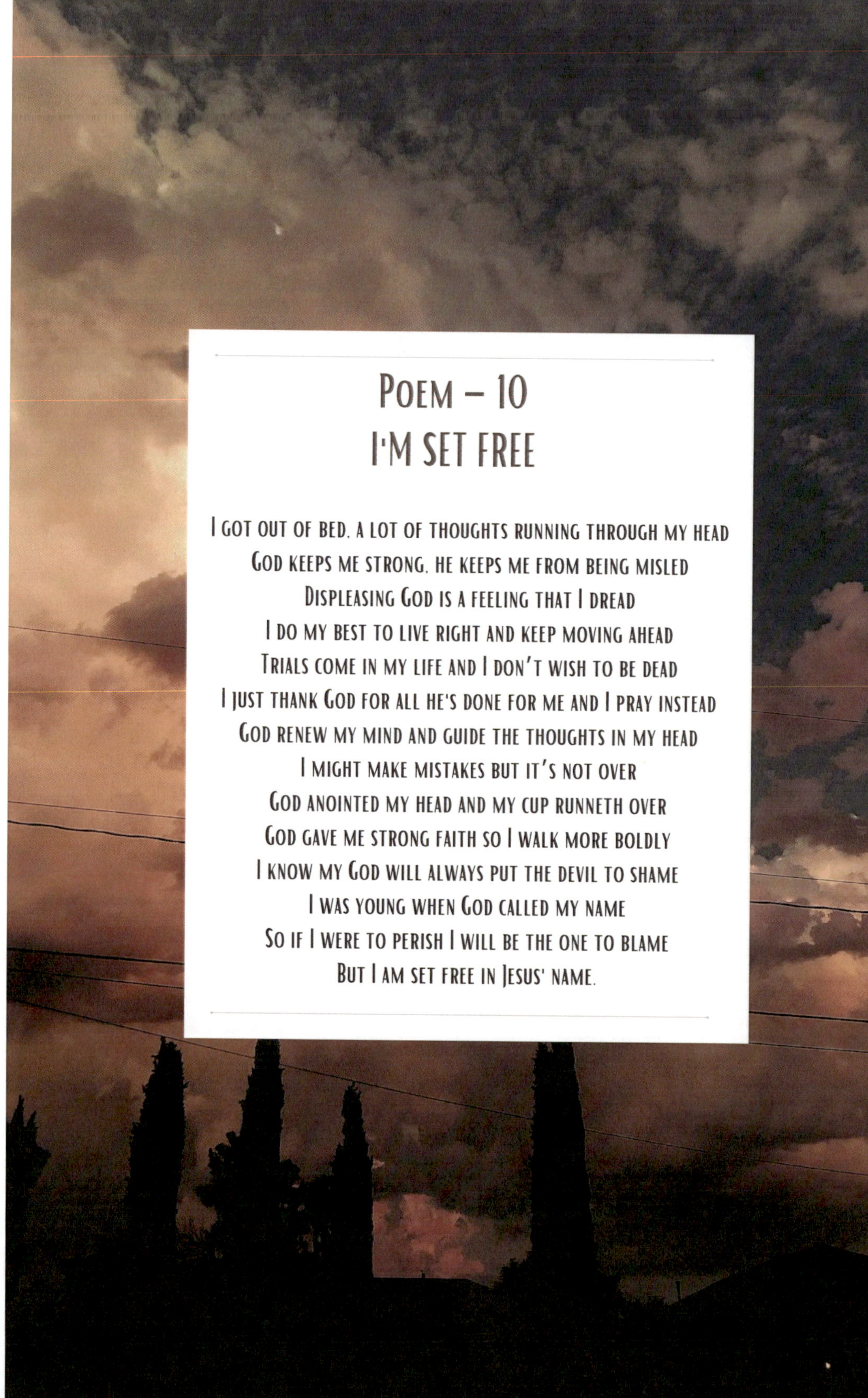

Poem – 10
I'M SET FREE

I got out of bed, a lot of thoughts running through my head
God keeps me strong, he keeps me from being misled
Displeasing God is a feeling that I dread
I do my best to live right and keep moving ahead
Trials come in my life and I don't wish to be dead
I just thank God for all he's done for me and I pray instead
God renew my mind and guide the thoughts in my head
I might make mistakes but it's not over
God anointed my head and my cup runneth over
God gave me strong faith so I walk more boldly
I know my God will always put the devil to shame
I was young when God called my name
So if I were to perish I will be the one to blame
But I am set free in Jesus' name.

GOD IS GOOD

It feels good to laugh and tell a joke
It gives you strength when you are down and
when you are broke
Listening to God's voice is as many waters as he
spoke
The Bible has many words that we quote
God is all-powerful, he can even heal you from a
stroke
He can cleanse cancer from your body and your
throat
I sing songs of praise and gasp to hold a note
If life were on the sea, God will keep me afloat
When God said let there be light there was light
as he spoke
God's presence is more comfortable than a
blanket or a coat
And his word cleanses us like water and soap.

A WONDERFUL PHRASE

I'm headed to the altar to give God some praise
I worshipped God for many years and many of my days
It took me a while but I'm finally saved
Living right for God is the lifestyle I craved
It's amazing how God works in mysterious ways
And sin was the cause of my horrible days
But God delivered me from the horrible phase
I was stuck in sin, living in a maze
And God brought me out as I reminisce
I sit here amazed
Jesus is king and that's a wonderful phrase.

TRIALS GIVE ME STRENGTH

Today I decided to spend time doing only what I truly like. I
wanted to share with you the insights of this experience. At
first, I didn't quite know where should I put my energy in. But
the I work hard, pressure doesn't fold me when I'm weak
God strengthens and he holds me, he brought me far from
the old me
God is the one that truly knows me
God takes me as far as I want to go
He made the summer, fall, and the winter snow
He predestined the height of how tall I would grow
He knows the future where the wind will touch before it blows
He gave us flexible bodies to reach our hands to our toes
That's something only a mighty God can do and know
No matter how far we go
God sits high and he looks low
He touches you with his spirit so his power in you can flow
Something that God lets us know
Is that the pressure in life is what causes us to grow.
magic happened. I became the most productive, loving and
inspired human being.

Poem – 13
TRIALS GIVE ME STRENGTH

I work hard, pressure doesn't fold me when I'm weak

God strengthens and he holds me, he brought me far from the old me

God is the one that truly knows me

God takes me as far as I want to go

He made the summer, fall, and the winter snow

He predestined the height of how tall I would grow

He knows the future where the wind will touch before it blows

He gave us flexible bodies to reach our hands to our toes

That's something only a mighty God can do and know

No matter how far we go

God sits high and he looks low

He touches you with his spirit so his power in you can flow

Something that God lets us know

Is that the pressure in life is what causes us to grow.

Poem – 14
THE DEVIL CAN'T WIN THE FIGHT

As the wolves howl into the moonlight
The caterpillar comes out of the cocoon into a butterfly at sunlight bright
In its wings and colorful in sight
Jesus be the light that carries me day and night
No need to fear, no need to be in fright
'Cause with God on my side the devil can't win the fight.

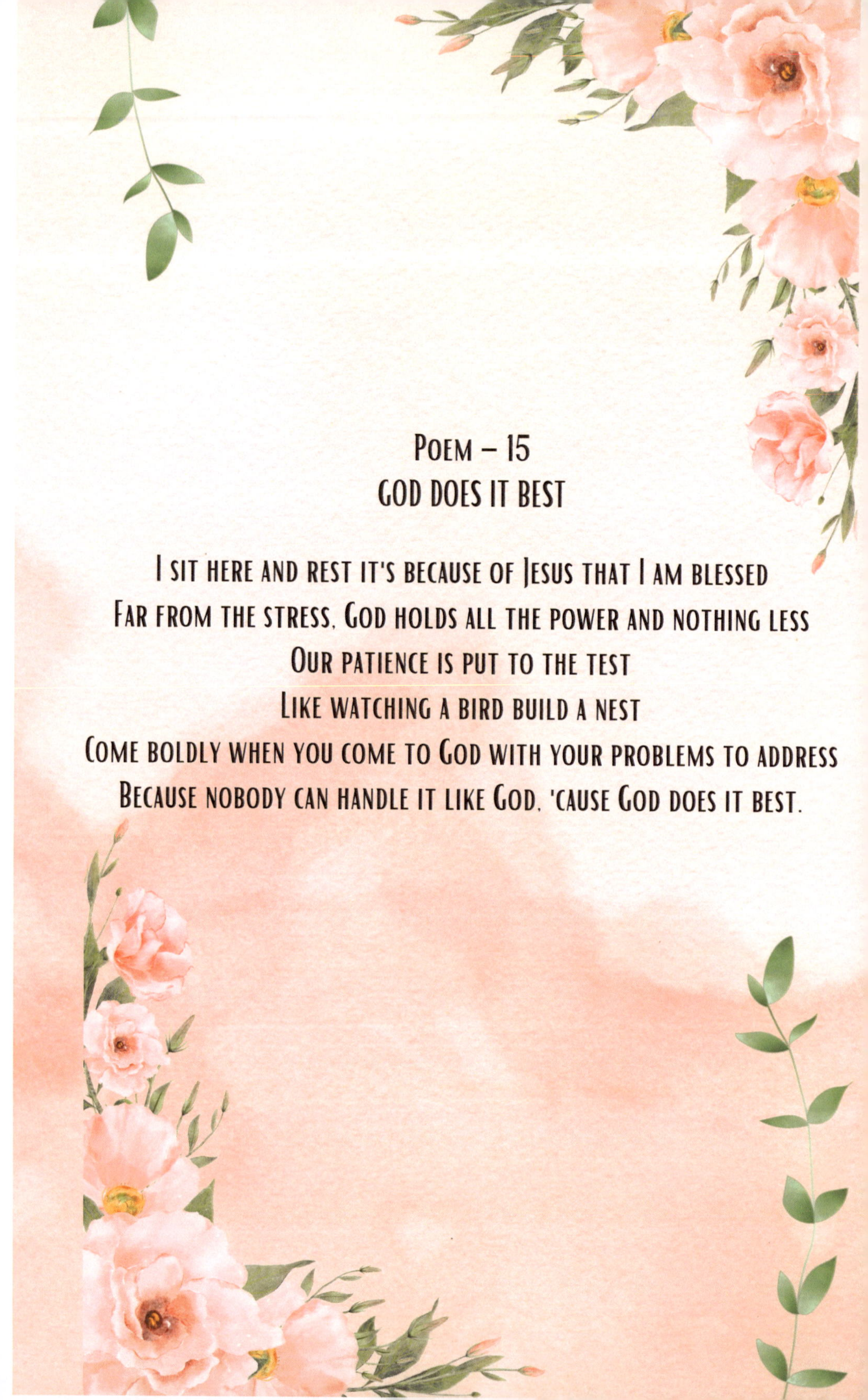

Poem – 15
GOD DOES IT BEST

I sit here and rest it's because of Jesus that I am blessed
Far from the stress, God holds all the power and nothing less
Our patience is put to the test
Like watching a bird build a nest
Come boldly when you come to God with your problems to address
Because nobody can handle it like God, 'cause God does it best.

Poem – 16
JESUS IS KING

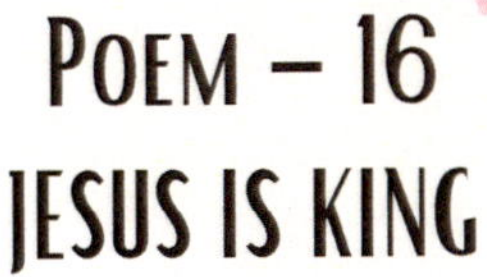

Jesus is king, ruler over everything
He made my soul clean, music is the gift God brings
Brought me out fresher than Irish spring
God does amazing things, he changed my whole scene
Gave me a spiritual vision in a dream
It's good to be on God's team
He covered me with his wing
Jesus is the reason my heart sings
He is brighter than a light beam
His spirit is where my soul clings
I'm just going in the direction wherever God moves or
leans
Casting demons out, you hear them scream
The demons were the reason I was mean
But Jesus delivered me from everything
And that's why Jesus is king.

Poem – 17
HOW I FEEL

Sometimes my mind is confused
God has given us power in prayer to use
So in battle against the enemy we will not lose
But there will be times that we fail
Just repent, take a deep breath, and inhale
Move forward just as the fisherman's boat sails
We overcome by our testimony
Because we all have a story to tell
To help someone escape the gates of hell
To strengthen the weak and encourage their
faith
So they don't walk around with a heart of hate
Jesus always said wise things as he spoke
Jesus is the reason why in the morning we
awake.

Poem – 18
We Are His Craft

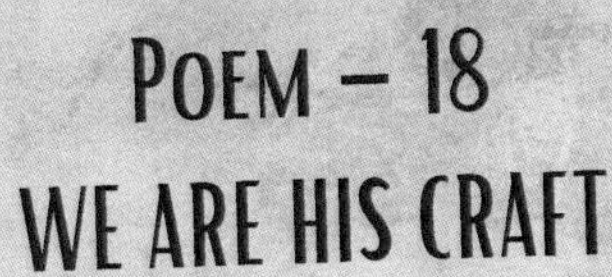

I'm taking you to Proverbs 19 and 8
And this is what the scripture states
"The one who gets wisdom loves life
The one who cherishes understanding will soon
prosper"
And that's the end of that scripture
In every situation make sure that God is in the mixture
Acknowledge God in all your ways
And he will direct your path
Give God all of you and don't give him your half
We are vessels for God, we are his staff
We want to live right, we don't want to feel God's
wrath
In living right Jesus speaks to the father on our behalf
God gives us joy, a taste of heaven when we laugh
God is the potter and we are his craft.

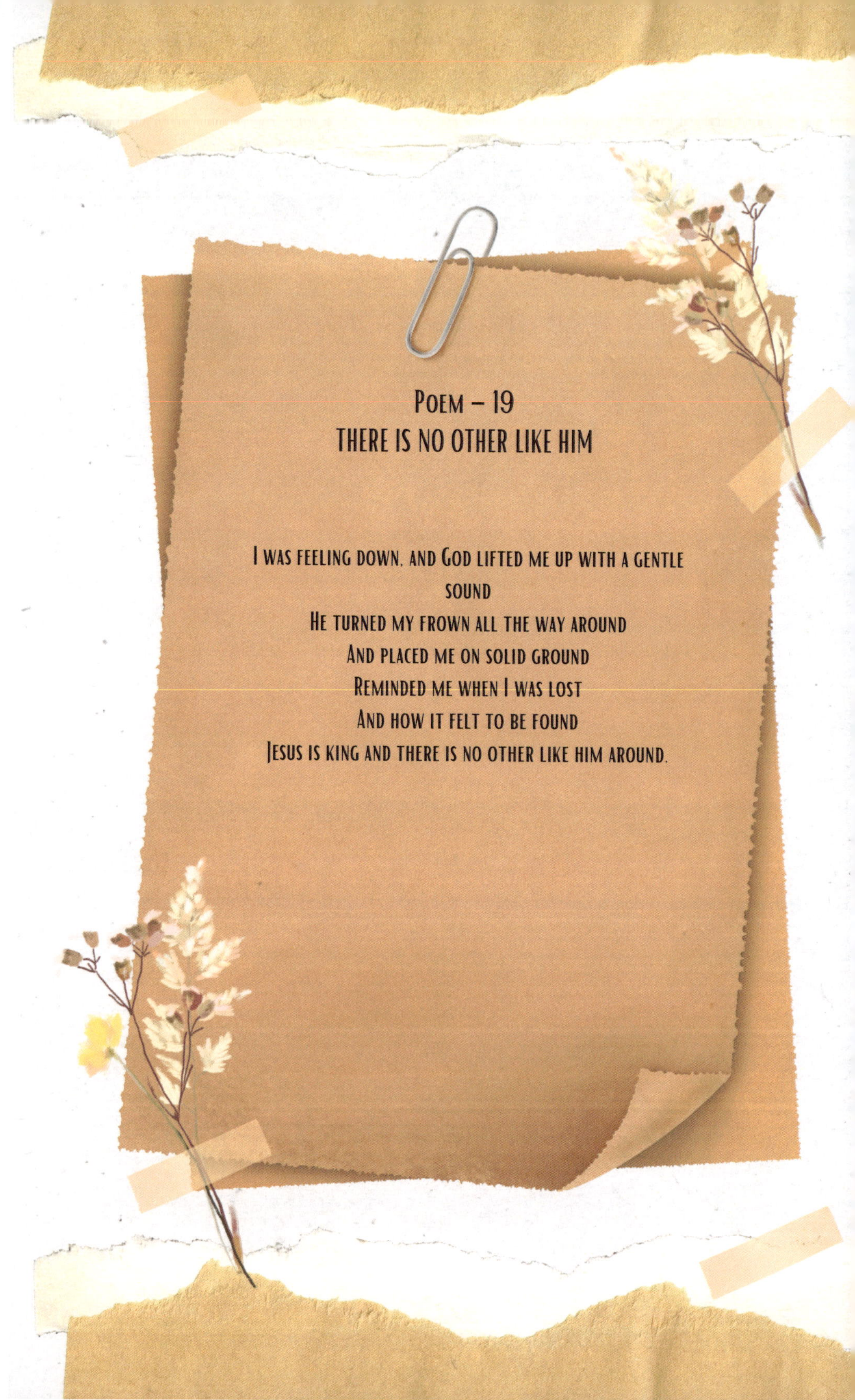

Poem – 19
THERE IS NO OTHER LIKE HIM

I was feeling down, and God lifted me up with a gentle
sound
He turned my frown all the way around
And placed me on solid ground
Reminded me when I was lost
And how it felt to be found
Jesus is king and there is no other like him around.

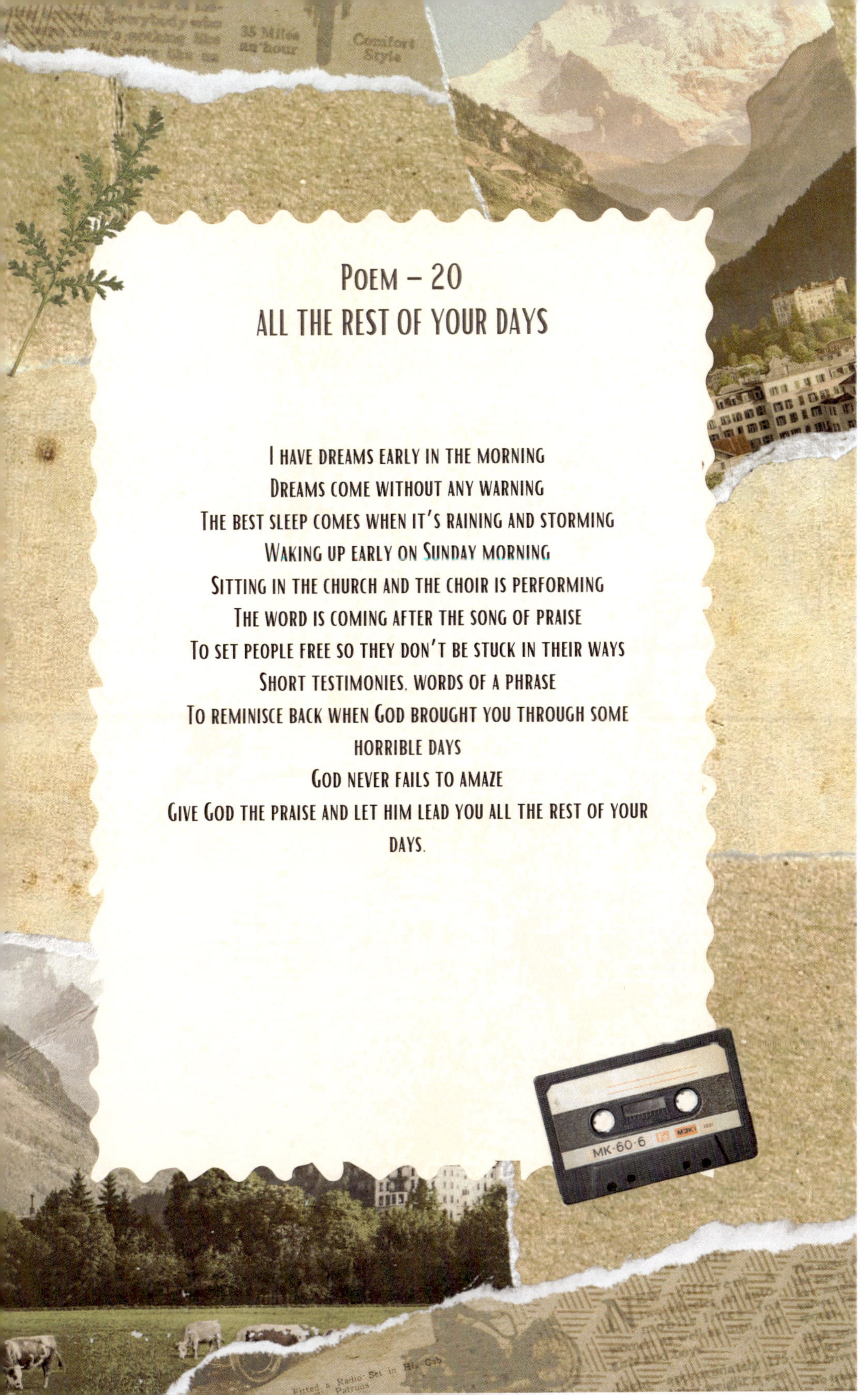

Poem – 20
ALL THE REST OF YOUR DAYS

I have dreams early in the morning
Dreams come without any warning
The best sleep comes when it's raining and storming
Waking up early on Sunday morning
Sitting in the church and the choir is performing
The word is coming after the song of praise
To set people free so they don't be stuck in their ways
Short testimonies, words of a phrase
To reminisce back when God brought you through some
horrible days
God never fails to amaze
Give God the praise and let him lead you all the rest of your
days.

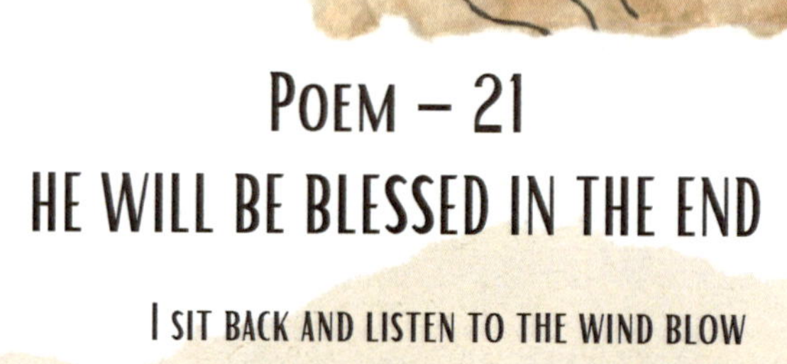

Poem – 21
HE WILL BE BLESSED IN THE END

I sit back and listen to the wind blow
Hearing the sound of a crow
While the sun touches my toe
Watching the waves of the river flow
My thoughts and my tomorrow only God will know
Some step into their calling fast and some walk into it slow
Keep your heart open so God can use you
And allow his spirit to flow
Casting out a demon, they have to leave when you tell them to go
The sun is bright and we are as white as snow
We search high and we look low
There is no other God like Jesus that I know
He is the first and the last, the beginning and the end
With true repentance, God forgives you of your sin
Help the poor, have a heart to lend
Live right before God and he will bless you in the end.

Poem – 22
LET HIM HANDLE IT HIS WAY

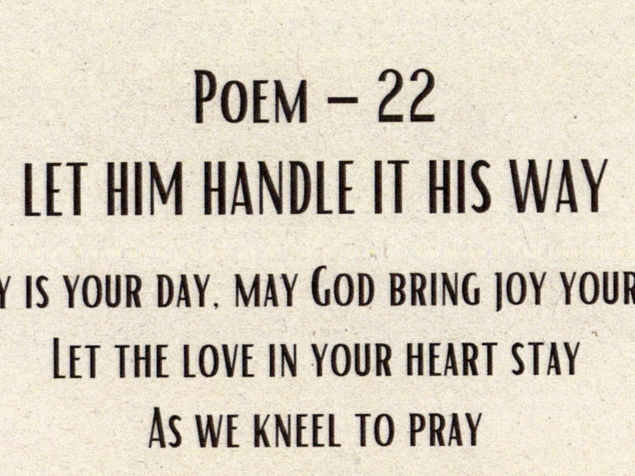

Today is your day, may God bring joy your way
Let the love in your heart stay
As we kneel to pray
Everything will be okay
Just let God handle it his way.

Poem – 23
I WON'T LET THIS OPPORTUNITY PASS ME BY

I see the sun in the sky shining bright in my eye
I see people dressed in a suit and tie for the
occasion. I don't know why
But I feel the Presence of God as I walk by
People came to greet me and say hi
And asked if I wanted to come to their event
but I was too shy
They asked me some questions and I didn't
want to lie
They were spiritual leaders in church with a
spiritual eye
They prophesied to me things that weren't a
lie
And invited me to church and I couldn't let
this opportunity pass me by.

Poem – 24
In God's Plan

I got grape juice in a can
I don't understand what's taking the cab so long
I could've taken a van or drove my father's sedan
My car has no fan but I thank God anyway
'Cause I'm still in his hand
The word is wrapped around my mind like a band
It's a nice day to go to the beach and lay in the sand
And let the sun hit my body and change my skin to a tan
I won't lay down long, eventually I will stand
No matter what comes my way all things work together
for the good in God's plan.

POEM – 25
WALK THROUGH HEAVEN'S GATE

Life is good, life is great
God, forgive me for my mistake
I was once lost but now I'm awake
God placed me at a table with food on my plate
I am not afraid if the earth will quake
If I am to die and it's my last breath, I take
My repentance through my life was for my
soul's sake
So when God calls me home, I can walk through
heaven's gate.

Poem – 26
BY GOD'S SIDE

---

*I don't have to hide, my God will always provide
Jesus stands by my side, his spirit is nationwide
For humanity Jesus died, the church is Jesus' bride
He will never wash us away through the ocean tide
Never commit suicide because Jesus stood in your
place and died
So that you may repent and have eternal life by God's
side.*

Poem – 27
WORDS CAN'T EXPLAIN IT IN MY SPEECH

When the praises go up, the blessings come down
Surely Jesus' Presence is in every town
Instruments of praise, God hears and loves the sound
God is full of joy and his mercy abound
God calls us home and lifts our soul above ground
To eternal life where there is joy all around
Everyone is happy and nobody wears a frown
Dressed in fine material as we cross the water in our gown
To stand before the father and receive our crown
Every word out of his mouth is profound
As we go to enjoy the feast we see majesty from the south, north, west, and east
Surrounded by God's peace a shout of joy we release
As we have a seat where there are vegetables, fruit, and meat
Grateful words come out of our mouths as we speak
And Jesus is at the table as we laugh, talk, and eat
God loves us each, he is so amazing words can't explain it in my speech.

Poem – 28
GOD ADORES

It is a blessing to give to the poor
We should all go to the store
Because people are in need of more
Some are old, and bodies are sore
Some people's hearts feel hurt and torn
Give a word of encouragement and a
lending hand
To help someone who is weak to stand
And God will let your blessings pour over
you
Because helping the homeless and weak is
what God adores.

Poem – 29
GOD'S RADIATING POWER

Life's temptation, I try to restrain
Old mistakes were part of my pain
Too many thoughts running through my brain
I bow my head and call on Jesus' name
Because praying to God is how I maintain
Strength from heaven so I don't go insane
As I grow wiser and the wisdom I gain
A trip to heaven on a luxurious plane
Heaven is not the only place God's spirit remains
I feel it in my room as his power radiates as he came.

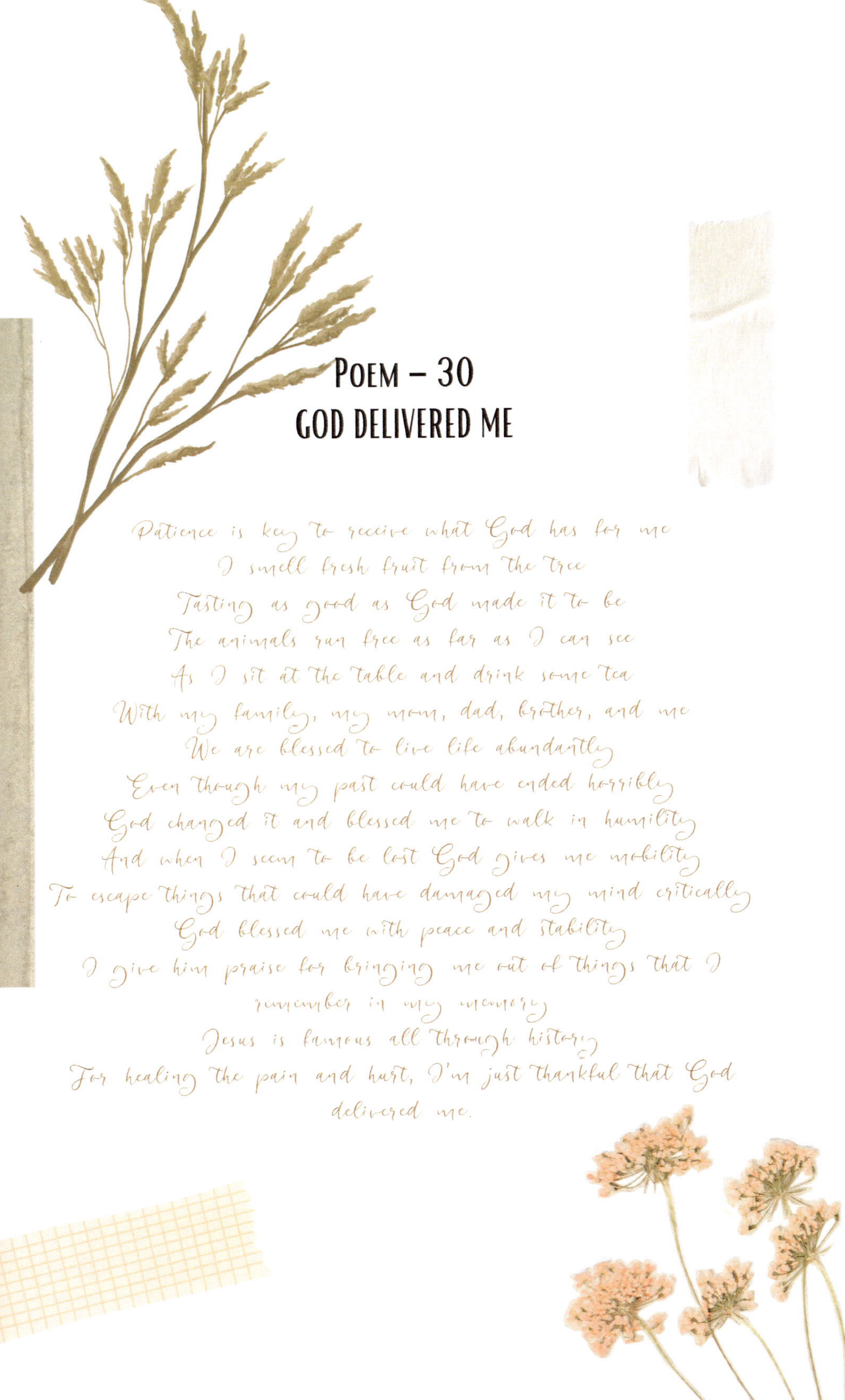

POEM – 30
GOD DELIVERED ME

Patience is key to receive what God has for me
I smell fresh fruit from the tree
Tasting as good as God made it to be
The animals run free as far as I can see
As I sit at the table and drink some tea
With my family, my mom, dad, brother, and me
We are blessed to live life abundantly
Even though my past could have ended horribly
God changed it and blessed me to walk in humility
And when I seem to be lost God gives me mobility
To escape things that could have damaged my mind critically
God blessed me with peace and stability
I give him praise for bringing me out of things that I
remember in my memory
Jesus is famous all through history
For healing the pain and hurt, I'm just thankful that God
delivered me.

Poem – 30
GOD DELIVERED ME

Patience is key to receive what God has for me
I smell fresh fruit from the tree
Tasting as good as God made it to be
The animals run free as far as I can see
As I sit at the table and drink some tea
With my family, my mom, dad, brother, and me
We are blessed to live life abundantly
Even though my past could have ended horribly
God changed it and blessed me to walk in humility
And when I seem to be lost God gives me mobility
To escape things that could have damaged my mind critically
God blessed me with peace and stability
I give him praise for bringing me out of things that I remember in my memory
Jesus is famous all through history
For healing the pain and hurt, I'm just thankful that God delivered me.

Poem – 31
BELIEVE IT

I am going to the finish line with nothing left behind
I'm done wasting time, God is the light that shines
He covers my mind and heals the blind
My soul is fine because the same God back then
Is the same God now in time
God is all-powerful, he can't be defeated
His holy fire hits your body and you feel preheated
God is just warming you up to preach the word in church
Where people are seated so you can tell them
And they can go out and repeat it for people to receive it
Our soul the devil can't retrieve it
Because of prayer and faith, the devil retreated
This is what happens when you trust in God so believe it.

Poem – 32
ENCOUNTERS THAT SOME PEOPLE HAVE

I sit back and think as I grab some water to drink
While I'm on my way to clean the dishes out the sink
I see a light in the corner of my eye as I blink
The water fell and I slid across the floor
As if I had on skates at a rink
The light approaches me as I begin to think
Wondering why it came so close
It was a different light from most
The being spoke with soothing waters like from the tide at the coast
Judging from this being's overwhelming presence
I knew it was the holy ghost
It was a surprising moment, to feel the joy was overwhelmingly real
As he said, "I love," and disappeared
While the atmosphere stayed peaceful and still.

Poem – 33
PARADISE TOGETHER

Words to write came in a thought
As I remember what my English teacher taught
While taking a walk with a cold bottle of water I brought
The Bible says your words should be seasoned with salt
Before I can say anything evil my words got caught
God put a doorkeeper over my mouth because I prayed that he would
The peace in the atmosphere was overwhelming as I stood
While I walked out of my room door with joy as I should
I grasp every thought in my mind that I could
And the only thing that I can think of was God is good
Jesus saved my life and changed me for the better
His presence is mighty and soft as a feather
I pray I be with God in heaven forever
And all my family make it in to enjoy paradise together.

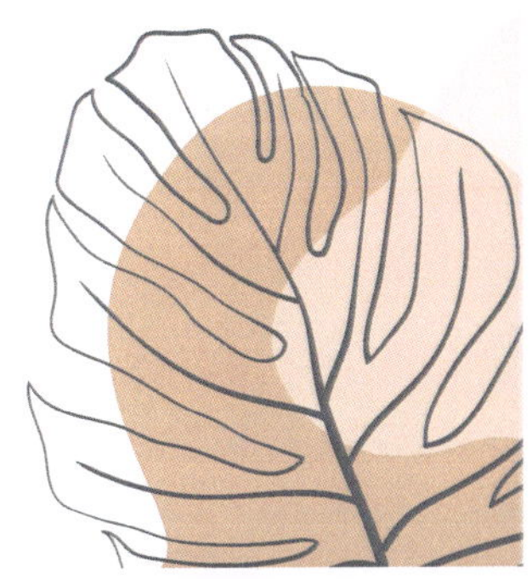

Poem – 34
Where I Belong

Sometimes I don't understand everything that God has
for me in his plan
I want to live right and never give up the fight
To make it into the light, I know my destiny is bright
I have faith in what I can't see in my sight
The word of God is what I hold onto tight
I know I will be alright, through prayer God puts the
devil to flight
And he gives me strength from day to night
To walk upright and to keep my attitude polite
God is like no other God, he is the God of light
He takes us through a storm to give us strength to be
strong
God knows there will be times that we feel we are alone
But God's peace is still as he sits on the throne
I choose Jesus because hell is not my home
I choose to live right so I can be in heaven where I
belong.

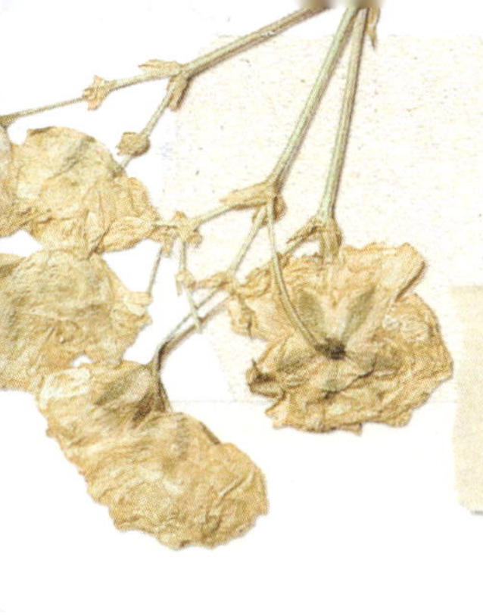

Poem – 35
GOD IS IN CONTROL

Times get hard and life seems to be a drainer
Sometimes I hide my feelings and emotions in a container
And I don't know what life would be like tomorrow
But I have a God that can take away my sorrow
And uplift my spirit. God's voice I wonder how it sounds to hear it
I know I will encounter his voice when I am near it
The devil tries to block my vision. He tries to smear it
I don't have to fear it because God is in control
And getting to heaven is the main goal
The journey is long and I will enjoy the stroll
God's presence is sweeter than a cinnamon roll
God gives me the strength to walk up bold
And he is the God of my soul. To see him will be amazing to behold
It's good to know that my God answers to no one. And he stays in control.

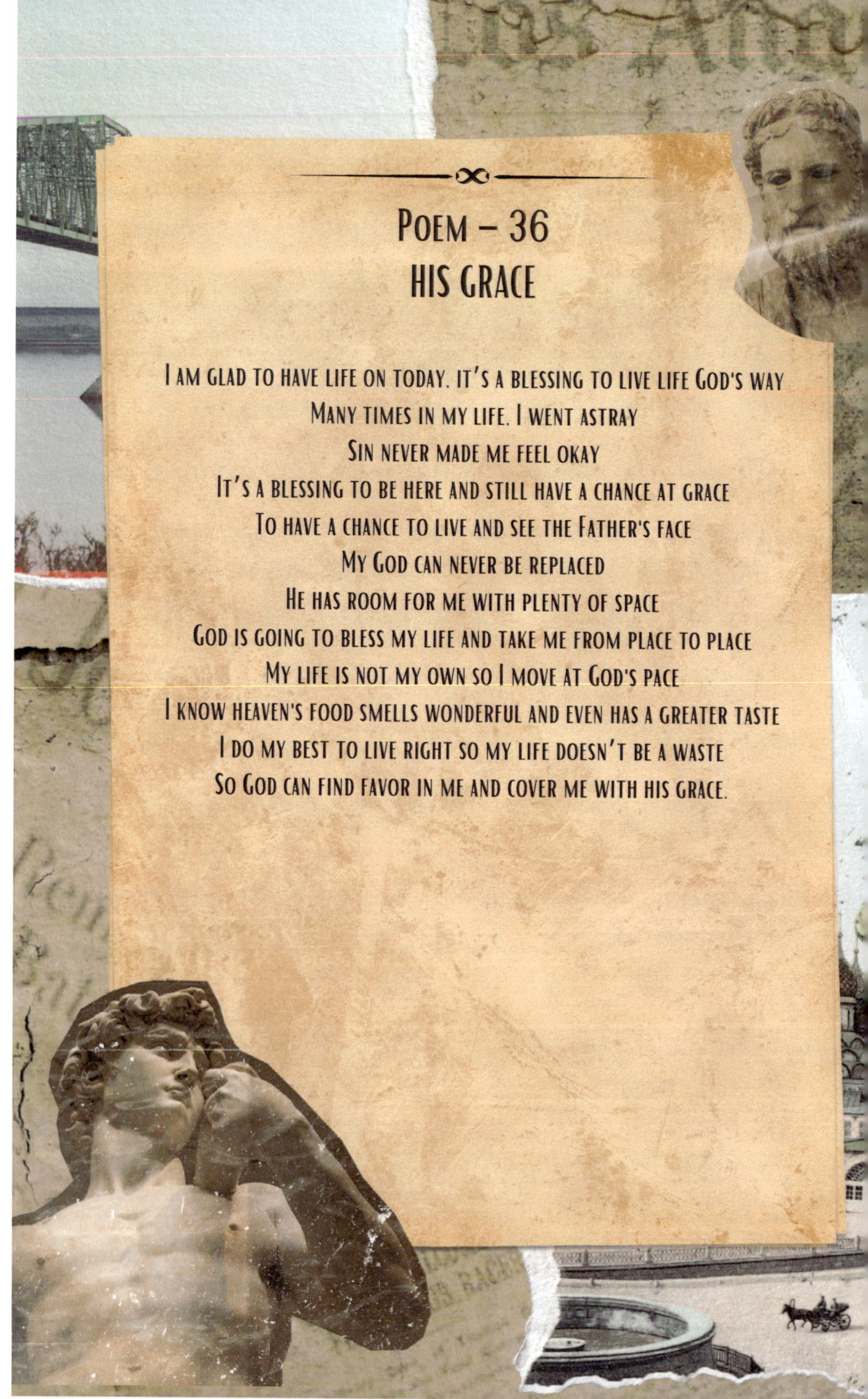

Poem – 36
HIS GRACE

I am glad to have life on today, it's a blessing to live life God's way
Many times in my life, I went astray
Sin never made me feel okay
It's a blessing to be here and still have a chance at grace
To have a chance to live and see the Father's face
My God can never be replaced
He has room for me with plenty of space
God is going to bless my life and take me from place to place
My life is not my own so I move at God's pace
I know heaven's food smells wonderful and even has a greater taste
I do my best to live right so my life doesn't be a waste
So God can find favor in me and cover me with his grace.

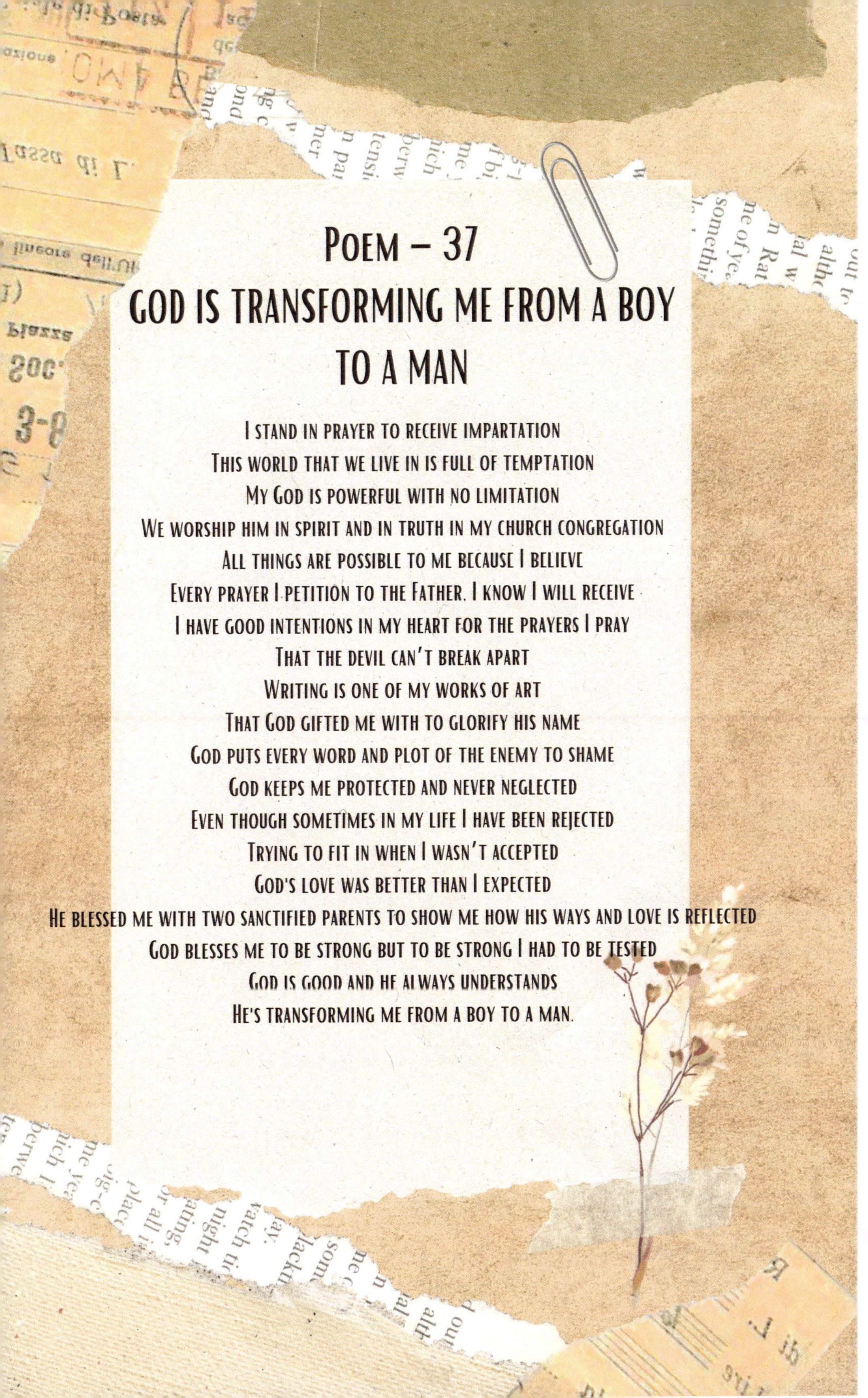

Poem – 37

God is transforming me from a boy to a man

I stand in prayer to receive impartation
This world that we live in is full of temptation
My God is powerful with no limitation
We worship him in spirit and in truth in my church congregation
All things are possible to me because I believe
Every prayer I petition to the Father, I know I will receive
I have good intentions in my heart for the prayers I pray
That the devil can't break apart
Writing is one of my works of art
That God gifted me with to glorify his name
God puts every word and plot of the enemy to shame
God keeps me protected and never neglected
Even though sometimes in my life I have been rejected
Trying to fit in when I wasn't accepted
God's love was better than I expected
He blessed me with two sanctified parents to show me how his ways and love is reflected
God blesses me to be strong but to be strong I had to be tested
God is good and he always understands
He's transforming me from a boy to a man.

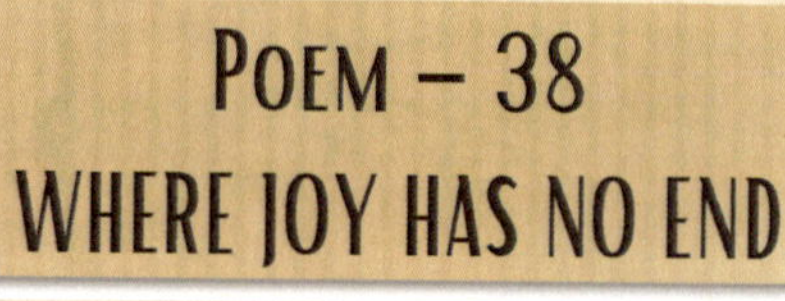

Poem – 38
Where Joy Has No End

My mind is settled and the old me is lost
I look outside to observe the winter frost
I can't wait till summer comes again
And the sun shines on me like God's presence with no end
God saved my life and freed me from sin
He directed my path when I didn't know where to begin
He is the same God that saved Daniel from the lion's den
God is so amazing I can't explain it all on paper and pen
Not even in words or ratings from one to ten
God never fails, he always wins
He blessed me with parents that can cook and afford
Cornish hen
And when I am in trouble or have an event they always
attend
My parents are my spiritual leaders and my closest kin
May God be with us all from the beginning into eternity
Where joy has no end.

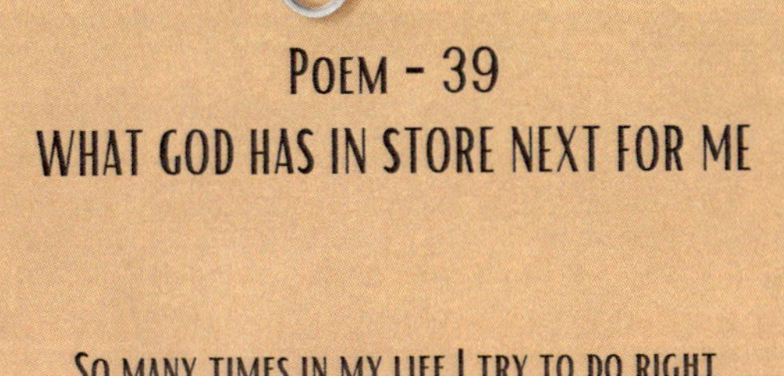

Poem - 39
WHAT GOD HAS IN STORE NEXT FOR ME

So many times in my life I try to do right
And trouble still comes but I know I'll be alright
Because God is where I get my strength from
Sometimes I complicate things but God still covers me with his wings
He sends me dreams, I am connected to his holy genes
I see images in my mind of success in different scenes
I dream every morning new dreams that God continually brings
I pray God help me interpret the dreams cause they are not always
what they seem
God's presence is sweet like pie and whip cream
God directs my path and leads me to my destiny
I know it's amazing what God has in store next for me.

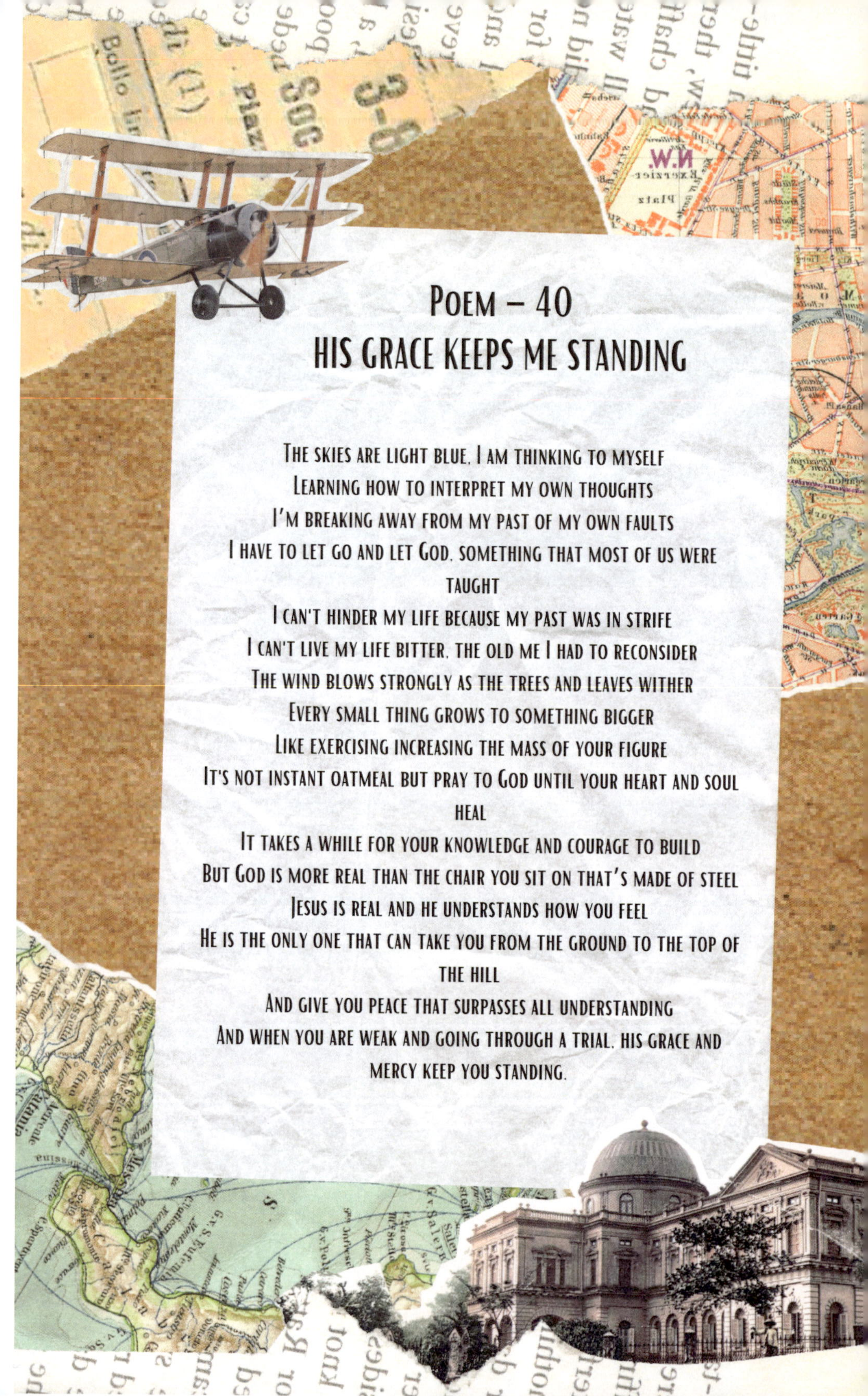

Poem – 40
HIS GRACE KEEPS ME STANDING

The skies are light blue, I am thinking to myself
Learning how to interpret my own thoughts
I'm breaking away from my past of my own faults
I have to let go and let God, something that most of us were taught
I can't hinder my life because my past was in strife
I can't live my life bitter, the old me I had to reconsider
The wind blows strongly as the trees and leaves wither
Every small thing grows to something bigger
Like exercising increasing the mass of your figure
It's not instant oatmeal but pray to God until your heart and soul heal
It takes a while for your knowledge and courage to build
But God is more real than the chair you sit on that's made of steel
Jesus is real and he understands how you feel
He is the only one that can take you from the ground to the top of the hill
And give you peace that surpasses all understanding
And when you are weak and going through a trial, his grace and mercy keep you standing.

Poem – 41
The Women God Has For Me

I sit and think in my mind
on how to do things better
and how to respond to things
in a way that is pleasing to God
I pray daily and I keep myself active
so I won't be lazy
I stare into the clouds
because they are beautiful and hazy
Waiting on the right woman
who is going to be the lucky lady
The woman to be my wife
The woman I'll love for life
The woman that will be in the kitchen
with the food and cut with the knife
The woman I argue with
and we come back together in peace after the strife
The woman that will give me chills
as if I was in a bucket of ice
The woman that will walk down the aisle
with a dress the color of rice
The woman I can eat cake with
and give her the last slice
The woman that's for me
and I don't have to gamble for her love like a game of
dice
The woman that loves me
that will make me say I do twice.

Poem – 42
He Is the God That Will Remain

Spring is here and summer is around the corner
The sun shines on the climate
as the cities are getting warmer
It got me feeling okay
My mom and dad have always been my protégé
They taught me how to keep Jesus first
every step along my way
That's the reason why I wake up every morning
to a brighter day
God teaches me how to fight against the enemy
like a sensei
He heals my broken heart and my pain
He fills my cup and lets it overflow with rain
He gives me understanding when I am confused in
my brain
He takes me to a higher level in life in a way I can't
explain
He strengthens me every minute and hour
He is in all control and he never runs out of power
He is a God that stays fresh and never goes sour
He is the God of my life, the God of every hour
The God of all power
The God like no other
The God that is closer than a brother
The God that put you in the womb of your mother
The God that created us to love each other
and praise his name
He is the God over all gods
He is the God that will remain.

Poem – 43
HE WISHES US WELL

How can I separate from the one who loves me the most
God will never leave my side, he is always close
He created the cow so we can be able to make the roast
We plant seeds in soil and out comes a rose
Beautiful in color and wonderful to smell in your nose
It gives you a get feeling from your head to your toes
What would life be without plants? Probably nothing I suppose
God made the earth and all the fine gold
He made us as people to worship him until we are old
And to spread the gospel to others to save their soul
We believers are courageous and bold
Our testimonies we must tell
to save the lost and keep them from hell
And by prayer, we can break the curses of a spell
Jesus is with me in my spirit, he dwells
He never gives up on me even though he knows
Sometimes I would fail
God is all merciful and he wishes us well.

Poem – 44
GOD'S PEACE IN MERCY WILL FOREVER ABOUND

God will make us the head and not the tail
For some, it may take a while
But just know that God is your pal
And he knows how to keep you with a smile
And his word will never go out of style
And his love is forever and not a short while
With God on your side, the devil can't win
He would throw in the towel
So give God the praise because he loves the sound
He will place your feet on solid ground
Where his peace and mercy will forever abound.

Poem – 45
IN YOU HE STANDS TALL

Pepper is not salt, it is pepper
And salt is not pepper, it is salt
So watch how you walk and talk
So you don't trip over your own fault
Watch what you entertain in your own thought
So you don't hinder your blessings that God brought
Don't be trapped in a world of sin and get caught
Because that's not the right way of life at all
Get on your knees and pray and give God a call
Because he can catch you before you fall
He can hear you in an open space
Or if you are surrounded by a wall
Our God is mighty and in you He stands tall.

Poem – 46
IN GOD'S LIGHT

I must settle down and pace my thoughts
Because a lot goes on in my mind
I was made unique, one of a kind
For God, I will always make time

For God is sweet like sugar
And the devil is as bitter as a lime
I know God will protect me in this world at all time
He will strengthen you in your heart, body, spirit, soul, and mind
He will keep you in line
And help you understand things that's hard to define
Don't stress yourself out to be perfect
Because putting all that stress on your mind is not worth it
God will perfect that which concerns us
And keep us from sin and worldly lust
Let God be the one in whom you put your trust
Because if you live right, your soul will go to heaven when your body turns to d
No need to live and be in fright
Because at the end of the day, God is the light
And God knows all you've seen in your days of sight
He knows what you will do and the things you thought you might
Keep living right and continue the good fight
Because God will put your enemies and worries to flight
And allow your future and destiny to shine bright
While you walk as a living testimony in God's light.

Poem – 47
HE NEVER LEFT ME

I've been feeling strange, trying to rearrange
Trying to get over this pain so I don't go insane
I read the Bible daily just to maintain
God is good always, I can't complain
I try to stay up in my lane
Dealing with somethings in my brain
Sometimes I feel drained
It's like I'm standing in the summer rain
And only God could take away the pain
The reason why it's feeling strange
Is because I'm living life for God and not for other things
Joy is the presence God brings
Life is not about me
But I have faith in what I can't see
It's about God and what he predestined me to be
Sometimes I go in the living room and talk to Uncle E
Sit back and laugh while we watch TV
I've been distant from people around me
And found out it was hard for me to find me
Until Jesus came alone and redirected me
I can't let the past keep affecting me
I was once blind but now I see
I was once in bondage but now I'm free
Jesus holds every key
He made me into a better me
Jesus saved me when I was lost
For me, he was nailed to the cross
God kept me and through my wrong, he never left me

Poem – 48
WE ARE HIS CREATIVE PIECE

The silence of my mind is peace
God's love for his people will never cease
It spreads from the north, south, and east
God is everywhere with his presence of peace
God's love fulfills us like food at a feast
God loves us like a dad loves his son
And an uncle loves his niece
God made the world and we are his most creative piece.

Poem – 49
SUMMER IS ALMOST HERE

Going out is fun. I am loving the feeling of the sun
The weather is getting nice and it's time for lots of water and ice
And seasoned food that tastes delightful with a touch of spice
And deep dish pizza that looks yummy and cheesy in every slice
I can't wait to start taking vacations at an affordable price
I just keep God first because he is the head of my life
He is the wisdom of my words and the speaker of my advice
Vacations may be a breeze
But it's the presence of God that keeps me at ease
Life is fun but trials can leave you stunned
But God is with me and his will, will be done
So I don't worry or fear about what I see or hear
God is always near so I am going to enjoy the life God has for me here
Through the pain, God caught my every tear
God has always been sincere
So I am going to enjoy life with no fear
Because God is the light of every season and year
So I am ready for my water and to hear laughter of cheer
Because the weather is getting nice and summer is almost here.

Poem – 50
HE CAN DO ALL THINGS

I am glad we are done with the snow
I knew spring was here when I heard the crow
The sun beaming from the sky and touching the earth low
It's time for flowers and vegetables to grow
I love sitting in church while the air conditioner blows
Touching everyone in their seated row
While the Holy Spirit flows with words of prophecy of things only God will know
God loves us so that he will never let us go
Even when we want to let ourselves go
God sits high and he covers us from below
His ways are not our ways, they are higher than we know
God will take your past and shame and turn it all around
Because you believe in Jesus' name
God will turn your pain to overflow blessings of rain
God will always provide, Lord I thank you for covering me with your wings
My God is like no other, he can do all things.

Poem – 51
What Do You Think?

God is good; he saved me from myself
When I felt low and alone
God was thinking of me as he sat on his throne
He is the healer of my soul and the creator of my flesh and bone
The universe my God created and he owns
He spoke it into existence with his voice in a powerful tone
When God spoke, the earth wavered for a few
As vegetables, plants, and trees grew
Herbs from the plants for our health
God made for us and not just himself
He gave us a brain to think
And made the ocean so we may have water to drink
God created all the colors from blue to pink
And gave us creativity to make a sink
And put a thought in our mind to skin an animal to make a coat of mink
God can change our lives instantly as quick as we could blink
Our God is amazing; what do you think?

Poem – 52
AWAKE

What God says will come and not pass
Like how he made the earth with green grass
Sometimes you have to be patient
Like when working out to build mass
Everything God does is in orderly fashion
It's not always fast
God gives us strength when we pray
He gives us peace when we rest to lay
God is an on-time God with a record of no delay
For his people. he has always made a way
He is the reason for my joy today
He is with me every day; he is never far away
Even when I used to go astray
God was patient with me until I came back his way
God made us to love and not to hate
God made cows for milk and tender steak
God is the knowledge in the things we create
He is the joy and the light when you walk through heaven's gate
He is the God that will never leave or forsake
He is the God of my soul that no devil can take
He is the God that hears my repentance and forgives me for my mistakes
He is the God of each morning that I awake.

Poem – 53
HE IS ALL I NEED

I stay to myself because I don't trust too many
My cup runneth over and my blessings are plenty
People showed hate but I didn't show any
People gave money advice and didn't share with me a penny
But God is for me; he is all I need
He nourished me to grow because in me he planted his seed
God takes his time and sometimes moves quickly in speed
God wants us to show love, so I am quick to do a good deed
God is the head of my life, and he is all I need.

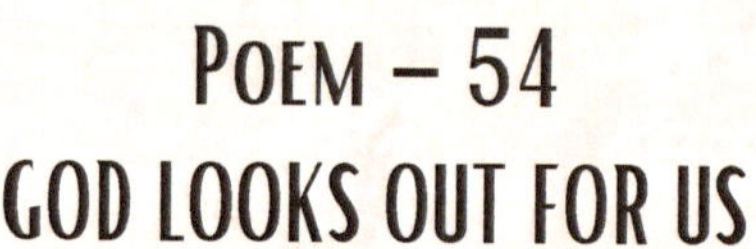

Poem – 54
GOD LOOKS OUT FOR US

To be free is to be untrapped in your mind
To be disciplined is to have order in how you spend your time
To have discernment is to read between the lines
To move forward is to ignore what's behind
To recognize warnings is to remember the familiar sign
Nobody likes the taste of a lemon or a lime
But every reader loves to read about a poet and his rhyme
To cross over from being of the world into God's path
Is a chance to make it into heaven and not feel God's wrath
God gives us strength to overcome and joy to laugh
God is with us, and he looks out for our behalf.

Poem – 55
UP TO HEAVEN WITH THE WIND

The wind is blowing through the trees and the grass
The wind is blowing toward your future and away from your past
The wind has been blowing since time began
God sent the wind to blow away your sin
The wind is spiritual and it has no end
With God in the afterlife, the wind blows again
God created the animals, the chicken, and the hen
And God's spirit is the joy of the summer wind
Good and evil in God's eyes don't blend
Because evil will die at the end
And the good God will take your soul up to heaven with the wind.

Poem – 56
THERE IS POWER IN EL SHADDAI

This troubles me, the pain of life
People go through a lot, and some are better off than others
Some people don't even trust their sister and their brother
Some grew up without a dad, just their mother
And we are judged not by our wrongs but by our color
We don't walk alone; we walk together
God wants us to love because that's how we make it better
We send off a letter to the post office and it gets to whoever
The mail was for, that's good teamwork
Like the body of Christ that the Lord adores
Through your problems, God is with you; he causes you to soar
The beauty of heaven will be amazing to explore
Put your trust in God and don't let the trials of life trouble you no more
God can fix your heart when life makes it feel torn
God can fulfill your hunger in your abdominal core
God can bless you to wake up rich and no longer be poor
He can take us from being low to high
And bless you with blessings from above the sky
And wipe your tears as we cry
Because there is power in El Shaddai.

Poem – 57
GOD SUPPLIES ALL MY NEEDS

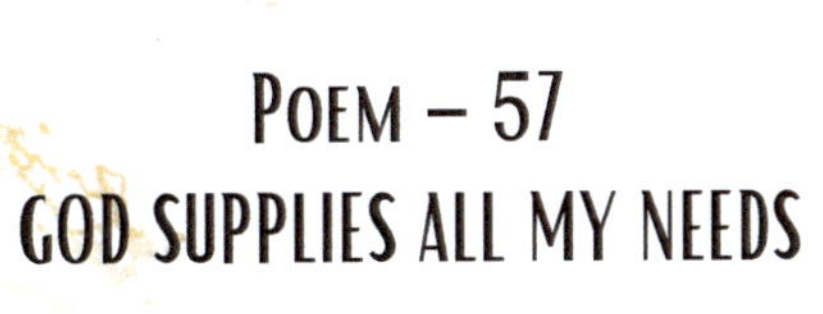

Lord, my heart was broken but by you I was chosen
My praise is real; it's from deep within of what I feel
You are the giver of the gift of my skill
You let the peace in my life stand still
You gave me the courage in my life I needed to build
Lord, I want to stay in your will
Your power is stronger than any prescription pill
Your words alone are strong enough to heal
The brokenness in the heart that your people feel
My blessings overflow and spill
To the way of your designed will
You are my everything, you are the risen king
Jesus, you are the key token to my heart no longer being broken
You are always with me; you never leave
In you, Jesus, I will always believe
Your Holy Spirit I have been waiting to receive
Your presence is sweeter than honey from the bees
And you are the supplier of all my needs.

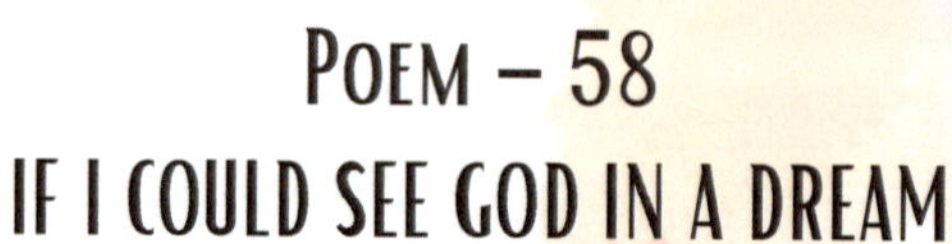

Poem – 58
If I could see God in a dream

To have a dream about God. I know everything will be amazing with no flaw
To see so much majesty more beautiful than anything on earth I ever saw
To run with the animals and not be bitten or scratched by their claw
To see God face to face will have me stunned with a dropped jaw
I believe God will say you can make it to heaven if you live right and follow my law
Keep the faith and don't grow weak because your time for blessings is at its peak
Continue to search. continue to seek
And one day again we will meet
Forever show love and watch how you speak
And let your attitude be clean like an area that is neat
This is a dream that will have me humble and meek
And wake up with lost for words to speak.

Poem – 59
TO SAVE MY LIFE

My thoughts are jumping off the wall
In my happiest and lowest moments, Jesus is who I call
Who else is going to catch me when I fall
When I am feeling weak, the God within me stands tall
He heals my pain: no need for a Tylenol
I am grateful for God's keeping power; he is with me all day not just for an hour
I thank God for soap and hot water for a shower
The name of the Lord is a strong tower
God's voice speaks clearly over everyone
Nobody else can do what God has done
He gave his only begotten son
So that we may have life; Jesus made the greatest sacrifice
His presence is more peaceful than the breeze of summer when it's nice
He is the refreshing cup of water and ice
He fills me with joy; that he paid the price
For someone like me to save my life.

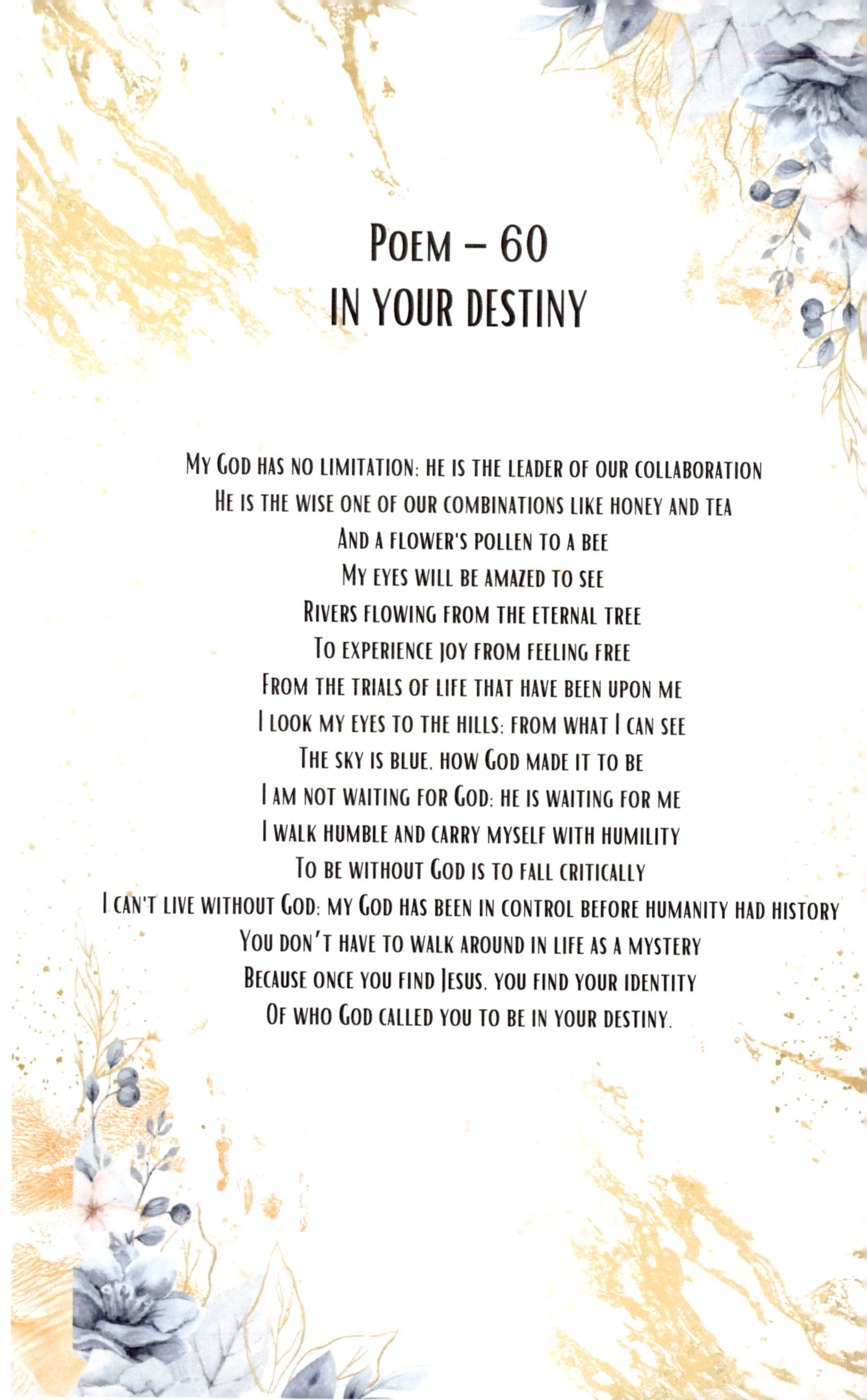

Poem – 60
IN YOUR DESTINY

My God has no limitation: he is the leader of our collaboration
He is the wise one of our combinations like honey and tea
And a flower's pollen to a bee
My eyes will be amazed to see
Rivers flowing from the eternal tree
To experience joy from feeling free
From the trials of life that have been upon me
I look my eyes to the hills: from what I can see
The sky is blue, how God made it to be
I am not waiting for God: he is waiting for me
I walk humble and carry myself with humility
To be without God is to fall critically
I can't live without God: my God has been in control before humanity had history
You don't have to walk around in life as a mystery
Because once you find Jesus, you find your identity
Of who God called you to be in your destiny.

Poem – 61
My God Can Bless You Wherever You Are

My God is not far
Even though heaven is above the shining star
God knows where you are
He is closer than you think; he is the living water
That fills your spirit more than the water you drink
He is the light that gives your eyes sight
He is the warm breeze of the summer night
He is the pilot of your destiny flight
He is the one who moves on your behalf when you can no longer fight
He is the God that is invisible to some but stands around in plain sight
My God has not given me a spirit of fright
But of power that worketh in me through his might
My God is not far; he can take away your painful scar
And bless you wherever you are.

POEM – 62
THAT'S WHAT I BELIEVE WHEN I LOOK UP TO THE SKY

I look up to the sky with limited vision of what I can see with my eye
I know that God is above the sky, and he feels every tear I cry
He has all the answers to my why
He is the life of earth's supply
He is the wings that cause me to fly
He is the God of light that can never die
He is bright like the sky from morning to night
He gives vision to my sight
He has the words to say to bring life into your day
So I look up to the sky as blessings come my way
I don't have to ask how or why
But I know God won't pass me by
Because I am the apple of his eye
That's what I believe when I look up to the sky.

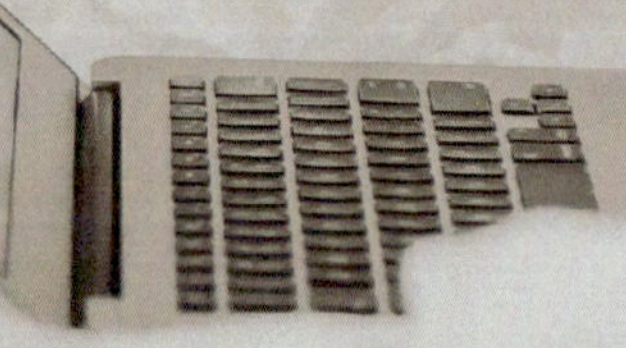

Poem – 63
AS THE WIND BLOWS

As I sit and listen to the wind blow
In the atmosphere of nature as the day begins to grow
Feeling the air of the breeze that blows through the flowers and the leaves
Causing my nose to sneeze
While I watch the branches sway from the trees
And disturb the hives of the bees
Where honey is hidden that no one sees
But God supplies all my needs
God is who I trust
So when my body dies and turns to dust
Up in the air my soul goes
As God uses the wind to lead me as it blows.

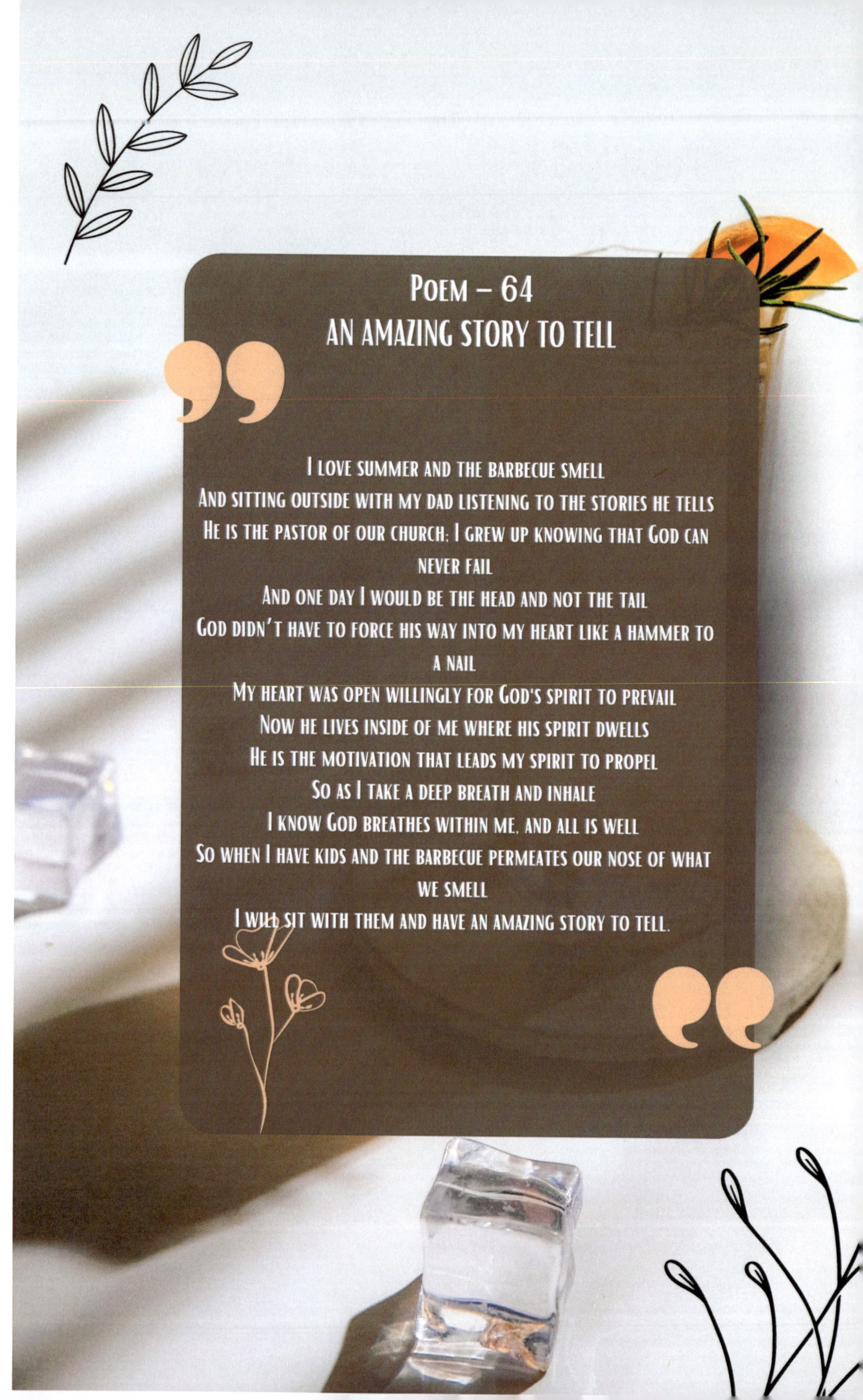

Poem – 64
AN AMAZING STORY TO TELL

I love summer and the barbecue smell
And sitting outside with my dad listening to the stories he tells
He is the pastor of our church; I grew up knowing that God can never fail
And one day I would be the head and not the tail
God didn't have to force his way into my heart like a hammer to a nail
My heart was open willingly for God's spirit to prevail
Now he lives inside of me where his spirit dwells
He is the motivation that leads my spirit to propel
So as I take a deep breath and inhale
I know God breathes within me, and all is well
So when I have kids and the barbecue permeates our nose of what we smell
I will sit with them and have an amazing story to tell.

Poem – 65
Speak Change in the Atmosphere

> " I speak life into the atmosphere
> I can feel my blessings about to appear
> I am blessed in this year
> My destiny shines bright and clear
> I am stunned by God's presence like
> headlights to a deer
> I speak from the heart when I pray to God
> sincere
> He listens to my voice, and I know he hears
> I open up my heart for God to speak into
> my ear
> I might not feel him all the time, but I know
> he is near
> To help carry me through to another year
> As life and death come from what you say
> and hear
> I just use the power God gave me to speak
> change in the atmosphere. "

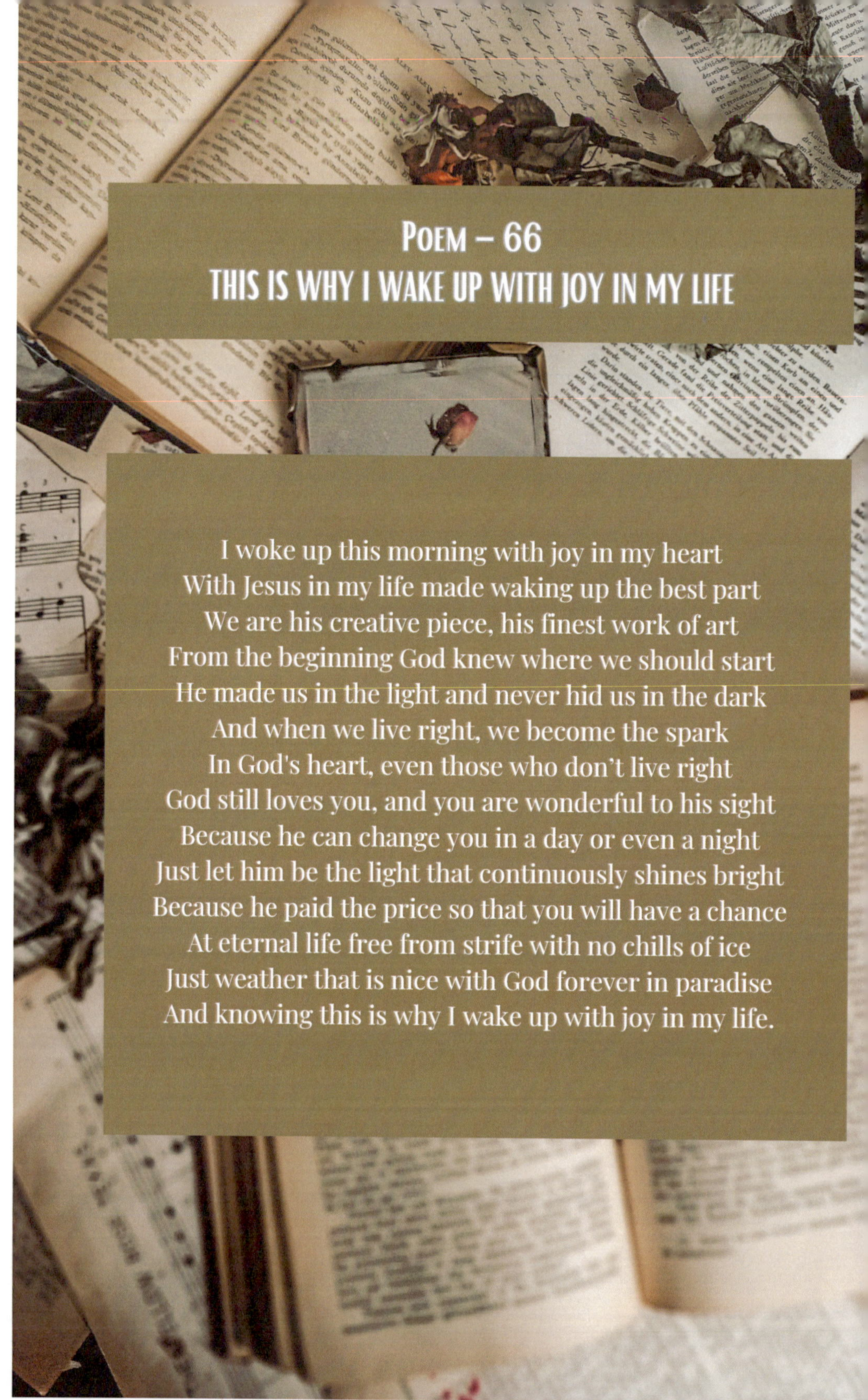

Poem – 66
THIS IS WHY I WAKE UP WITH JOY IN MY LIFE

I woke up this morning with joy in my heart
With Jesus in my life made waking up the best part
We are his creative piece, his finest work of art
From the beginning God knew where we should start
He made us in the light and never hid us in the dark
And when we live right, we become the spark
In God's heart, even those who don't live right
God still loves you, and you are wonderful to his sight
Because he can change you in a day or even a night
Just let him be the light that continuously shines bright
Because he paid the price so that you will have a chance
At eternal life free from strife with no chills of ice
Just weather that is nice with God forever in paradise
And knowing this is why I wake up with joy in my life.

Poem – 67
WHEN I DIE

When I die, grace is what I behold
Being with God is richer than gold
His love is joy like a father seeing his boy
God is with me all the time, my body is behind
But my soul is fine, 'cause through my life
God kept me in mind, in my wrongful phase
I stand amazed as God sits on the throne
And I have no words to phrase
God catches my gaze and the wind suddenly feels like a wave
I will open my mouth and give him praise
For how he kept me through all of my days
The God of wonderful ways, the God that never fails to amaze
As I look up to the skies, heaven is above
The clouds in disguise, the Bible I read to memorize
So I can live right and have eternal life as my prize.

Poem – 68
Where the Clouds Seem to be Grey

Sometimes I feel lazy and sometimes I feel strong
But I push myself in the right direction while God moves me
Around the devil's deception so I can grow in progression
As God gives me a life of correction
As I humble myself and listen to the choir selection
I have high expectations, knowing that God will bless me
With an organization to be a help to those that are in need
And put a smile on his face from my good deed
I work on patience so I don't move in speed
I just let God's Holy Spirit guide me as he leads
Being strong is what takes the laziness out of my day
I thank God for always making a way
Because he lives within me where his Holy Spirit stays
And he shines the light where the clouds seem to be grey.

9 798869 350374